HEALED AND UNLIMITED

₪ ₪ ₪

The Secret To Breaking Free
FROM CHRONIC DIS-EASE AND
IGNITING PERSONAL POWER

₪ ₪ ₪

Martha G. Blessing, RN

DISCLAIMER: This book is not intended as a substitute for the medical advice of a physician. The reader should regularly consult a physician in matters relating to his/her health and particularly with respect to any symptoms that may require diagnosis or medical attention. You should never delay seeking medical advice, disregard medical advice, or discontinue medical treatment because of information in this book. The author assumes no responsibility, legal or otherwise for any opinions expressed in this book.

₪

This book is dedicated to my father, George, always my best friend, for his undying love and support of my life and my dreams in this life and beyond. To my friend, Joe, who encouraged me to believe in the magic of life and taught me how to spread my wings and fly in the face of fear. It is dedicated with all my heart to anyone living with chronic pain or illness seeking to find their way back to health and vitality.

₪

TABLE OF CONTENTS

PREFACE

How is it we have come to believe that our bodies are going to break down and turn against us? How have we come to live in fear of inevitable pain and illness? For years I told my story of healing to people who crossed my path in an effort to inspire them. I wanted them to have hope and to believe in a possibility of healing their pain-stricken bodies. I believed deep in my heart that anyone could do the same thing that I did. I believed that I had emerged victoriously from ten years of chronic pain for some sort of higher purpose. Today, I know that as a deep truth. I am deeply blessed and grateful for the knowledge, insight, and wisdom gained from looking in the rearview mirror to those years when my body and life were consumed with chronic pain.

Every time I told my story people would say, "You should write a book. This could help a lot of people." I couldn't agree more. And yet, what I believe to be the *truth* about what really changed my circumstances and allowed me to create a thriving life and pain-free body is not what many want to accept as reality. My health and healing did not come from Western medicine or science. Back then when I told my story, it was always the abridged version. I told the one that I felt people could understand and accept. I told the story that was safe. It was just easier that way. Leaving out the spiritual and mystical details made *me* feel more comfortable. But years later I realized that not to tell the complete story is an injustice to me, to God, and to humanity.

There are many books written by "credentialed" medical professionals that offer tangible, scientific solutions for pain *management*, viewing it as a physical medical problem. Of late, there are even books that address pain management from a "holistic" perspective. Yet my belief is that if these books and modalities are "truth," then they should be successful and effective at eliminating pain, rather than just managing it. So I ask you—why are there still millions of people living with chronic pain? Why are there millions of victims succumbing to chronic pain and illness, along with its crippling financial woes and mental and emotional depression, flooding medical offices and hospitals in desperation? Why are there thousands, maybe even millions, of people tragically addicted to prescription narcotic pain killers, who move on to become addicts of street drugs like heroin?

This was my burning question and driving force for well over ten years. Why do some people heal and others don't, not just from pain but from other illnesses as well? Why was I able to break free, completely free, from ten years of chronic pain and fibromyalgia without a trace of residual effects, and why are there still so many people not able to heal?

It was a question that would take me nearly twenty years to answer. In my journey to reveal an answer, I came to have a mantra—"the Universe is always saying *yes*"—and so I would continue to ask the questions, trusting that the answer would be revealed to me. In hindsight I see that every single aspect of my life thus far has been for me to get a full resolution and answer to this question.

I believe that this book is not like any other book you will read about pain relief. It is not a book about how to live with pain and manage it. This is a story about living with pain and how I came to know and believe that I could reverse it and live a life of joy, health, and vitality…without it.

It would be grandiose for me to claim that I have all the answers for every person living with pain. But what I can do is tell you my story and show you the steps I took to reverse fibromyalgia and other chronic pain. I can teach you the principles that I gleaned and used to change my health and improve my life. I can tell you that some of these tools and principles may seem so simple and enigmatic that you could be tempted to overlook them.

I have come to know and understand that I was not given some kind of favor or special treatment by "God" or life that allowed me but not others to heal. It just isn't true that I was born with something *more* or *better* inside of me that made it possible for me, or that others are destined to live with chronic daily pain or illness.

I believe that every human being can live without chronic back pain, fibromyalgia, sciatica, arthritis, diabetes, and the like. I believe it is our birthright and divine plan to live without chronic illness or disease. Most will say that is a *tall order*, but I believe that no matter how severe, it can be healed. I have been witness to it, so it *is* my reality. I believe that illness is a learned experience and that we can unlearn it. This is the true and honest story that I will tell. I will tell you the unabridged version in which I unlearned pain. I will tell you the mystical spiritual truth and the one that I believe challenges everything that we've been told about pain, illness, medicine, and healing.

It is my true desire that if my story saves one person from becoming an addict to prescription drugs or heroin, or helps even one person reverse chronic pain and to move away from being a victim, then I have served in writing this book.

INTRODUCTION

Definition of insanity: doing the same thing over and over and expecting to get different results. ~Albert Einstein

WHY YOU NEED THIS INFORMATION

Y ou need this information because it is not available from the average Western medical doctors. ABC News reports that in America alone, 116 million people live each day with chronic pain with little hope for relief. If you are one of these people, you should know it doesn't have to be this way. I healed from ten years of chronic and debilitating pain, and I believe you can too.

Despite what the media portrays, you were born with an innate and organized healing system. Your body is equipped with the wisdom to self-heal and return to a state of health, wholeness, and vitality. Unfortunately, most of the treatment methods for pain only attempt to cover up the symptoms rather than address the underlying cause. Modern medicine has yet to dig deeper to address the root cause of the problem. I know you may be thinking: I know the cause of my pain—it's fibromyalgia or a slipped disc or rheumatoid arthritis.

But have you ever asked yourself why? Where did all these illnesses and diagnoses come from? Modern medicine often tries to point to genetics. No one in my family ever had back problems before I did. No one in my family ever had fibromyalgia. So I still have to ask: Where did this come from? What is the root cause? How did I come to be diagnosed with "degenerative disc disease" at 28 years old? I was an active, fit, young woman, a competitive figure skater for much of my life. My body was muscular, toned, strong, and well developed. How could I have a degenerative disease at 28 years old? Was that really the cause? Why would my body be degenerating at only 28 years old? It certainly wasn't genetic. No one in my family had this. Did I really believe in a body that was programmed to break down at 28 years old? That had not been my experience thus far.

Modern medicine has come a long way, but in my opinion it has missed the mark with its inability to develop intuitive truthful relationships with patients in the current "sick care" system. Nowadays we hear the terms "integrative" or "holistic" medicine, but what are they really? We hear talk about a body-mind-spirit approach, but how many patients feel comfortable about discussing or addressing mental, emotional, or spiritual aspects of their lives with their doctors?

And how many doctors have the desire or time to listen to these aspects of their patients' lives? How many doctors feel equipped or comfortable even hearing, let alone addressing, these sorts of aspects of their patients' lives? It scares most of them because it can't be measured quantitatively. It is an area in which insurance companies and the science of medicine feel uncomfortable. Mental and emotional aspects of a patient's health and well-being are addressed in the realm of psychiatry, but never in the area of pain management. There is a separation of the mind and body in specialty areas in Western medicine, despite all attempts to become politically correct to the demands of consumers.

Most physicians are unfamiliar with a truly holistic approach. They have forgotten how to treat each patient as a whole as the insurgence of managed-care medicine becomes a numbers game between providers and insurance companies. They manage and treat symptoms, not people. They treat illnesses instead of people. Many doctors even have a financial interest in the pharmaceutical therapies they prescribe. With the rise of managed health care came the popularity of the specialist. A different doctor for each health concern makes for segregated, not integrative, health care. Hello? Our body, mind, and spirit are not separate. They are all *housed* in one place, in this thing we call *the body*. Our bodies are an interactive energetic feedback system. In order to effect healing, a patient must be viewed as an entire system, not just a set of symptoms.

From a place of fear, many doctors are trained to answer to, and comply with, insurance company standards of care, ordering unnecessary tests to protect themselves from lawsuits and malpractice claims. This has set a code and standard for the insurance and medical industries, but it has done nothing to improve the results that a patient receives when seeking healing from chronic illness. And so it is that we have come to let these two industries tell us that we can and should be "okay" with being managed, that we should accept management of symptoms. From the moment I entered nursing school and took my first anatomy and physiology class, I was amazed at the wisdom and ability of the human body to function properly as a *well-oiled machine*. What goes on behind the scenes is truly miraculous, every single day. It never occurred to me as a nurse or a consumer that I would want to be "okay" with just managing illness. When I entered nursing school it was with the intent to improve my patients' lives and to lessen pain and suffering. How have we come to believe that our bodies are going to break down or turn against us? How have we come to believe that managing symptoms and managed care are the only options?

It takes little effort to see that around the world many of our health care systems are costing more and providing less. I challenge any consumer to watch a television program in its entirety without seeing paid advertising for prescription medication. Pharmaceutical companies have inundated our "programming," not just on our televisions, but in our belief systems too. With massive campaigns in magazines and on televisions, consumers are now trained in Western culture to "check with your doctor to see if (fill-in-the-blank) medication is right for you," while millions continue to suffer with symptoms of chronic illness and pain.

Consumers in recent years have begun to demand and search out other options. They have started to ask the same questions that I began asking some 20+ years ago. As best as I can see it, Western medicine offers solutions for management of symptoms, not freedom from them. Even *holistic care* is missing the mark. Why? Why are holistic medicine and the body-mind-spirit approach still not producing success and results for most people? I'll address that later in this book. It's a very important piece of the puzzle.

What I propose is a life free from physical pain and illness. I have found it and I wholeheartedly believe that it is possible for thousands, if not millions, of people if they are willing to explore the concepts that I present here.

You don't have to suffer with chronic pain or the side effects of medications and narcotics. You can live a life free from pain. You need this information because it is not available from most medical doctors or even holistic practitioners.

THIS WILL HELP YOU HELP OTHERS

If you are willing to accept 100 percent responsibility for yourself and the outcome of your health, and you use the information and tools in this book, you will start to feel better. You will remember what it was like to live a happy and joyful life in a body without pain. You will recover your life and your spirit. You will feel lighter and clearer as the side effects of medications wear off.

As you begin to heal you may notice something interesting happen in your life. You'll find that people who you can help will come into your life. They'll be looking for answers and you will have them. This is a part of the tremendous paradigm shift that is happening in our world and it is changing how true health and care are coming back together with each other. I have been observing it as a nurse and spiritual teacher for well over 20 years. The power that was once perceived to be held only by doctors is being transferred to everyday folks. Plain old everyday people like you and me are being called to help others in ways that had previously only been considered in the realm of medicine. People who have come through the other side of pain or illness are teaching and helping others to do the same, not because there is a financial benefit or gain, but because they can share their experience and relieve the suffering of others. People are becoming empowered to take responsibility for the outcome of their long-term health, rather than be at the mercy of being *managed* by someone else.

I believe that many (as I was) are "given" their pain or illness in order to learn specific lessons and to share that wisdom with the rest of the world in order to help us all heal. If you are called, don't be surprised. You have answered a call to advance humanity. You are a gift and a blessing, and the reason for your pain will be revealed and healed.

I WANT TO HELP YOU

My intention is to share with you the tools and principles that led to my healing and the complete reversal of my pain and fibromyalgia, in the hopes that they may help you return to a state of peace, health, and happiness. There are certainly challenges in life, but you should know that you have an extraordinary life force within you that knows no limits. I imagine that if you are living with chronic pain or illness and have exhausted every hope with medicine, you may find this hard to believe or accept. Believe me, I get it! I've been there. But I'm going to ask you— How badly do you want a better life? I wanted it and I didn't stop until I got what I wanted.

You can learn to access your own unique healing energy. You can learn to access this life force and to direct it to reverse chronic illness or pain. Sounds too simple, doesn't it? I'm here to help you. I'm here to teach you the key to connecting to and using this divine energy and life force to unlock the door to health and healing. It is the energy that beats your heart with no effort from you. It is the energy that expands your lungs and fills them with air without you having to think about it.

I have dedicated the last 19 years of my life and my work to learn about and study this divine life force in its physical, mental, emotional, and spiritual state. I became a nurse because I wanted to help others who were sick. I wanted to help people get well. I could never imagine the path I would take that would help me to do this. My desire is the same but my destiny changed when I answered the call that was presented to me. I'm still amazed some days that my purpose is to teach others what I have learned so that they can live healthy, vibrant lives. I am excited that you're reading this book.

WHAT QUALIFIES ME TO OFFER GUIDANCE?

Some are challenged to accept that medical doctors don't have all the answers to resolve our physical illnesses. It is our social norm to reach for the phone to call a doctor to see "what's wrong" and to get a diagnosis. It's also much easier to give the responsibility to someone else. And yet, we continue to do so while watching the medical communities heal less and less illness and pain. We continue to see the rates of chronic illness and pain skyrocket, despite all of the supposed "breakthroughs" in medicine and science. Have you ever really stopped to ask yourself why?

Don't get me wrong—if I fall and break my leg or have an accident while driving my car, by all means, please take me to the hospital. I believe medicine is proficient with acute emergencies and life-saving interventions.

But when I set out to learn something, I want the most qualified teacher. I've always been that way. I want to know every aspect and I research all the possibilities. I want to learn from someone who has been on the frontlines, who has lived the ups and downs and the ins and outs of the subject I am studying, so I can learn from their lived experience, their successes, and possibly, their mistakes.

If you feel the same way I do then you understand that I am an expert in this field because I lived with the physical, mental, emotional, spiritual, and financial fallout of chronic pain. I am humbled, happy, and honored to say that those days are long ago behind me and I have moved from that life of pain and struggle to become a happy, healthy, and financially stable woman, thriving and in love with life itself!

No, I'm not a medical doctor with credentials to practice medicine. My credentials are: I completely recovered from debilitating and crippling back pain after an injury; I got myself out of a wheelchair when doctors said I would not walk; I recovered from three back surgeries; I recovered bowel and bladder function after they were lost; I weaned myself from narcotic pain pills after taking them for 12 years; I dug deep to find the answers that medicine didn't have to heal the symptoms of fibromyalgia and completely reverse them; in 2005 I began training to run a marathon; and I live without pain or illness.

I hope that you will begin to see your pain in a different light and with a glimmer of hope. Pain and illness may have taken its hold on your body, your mind, and your spirit, but it is never "too late" for a shift and for healing to occur. I believe in miracles and you should too. They happen every day. You don't have to earn yours. You simply have to allow it.

I've had excruciatingly painful needles put into my neck and spine to deliver medicine directly into my spinal fluid in an attempt to heal fibromyalgia. I've had surgeries and procedures cancelled just hours before the facilities were shut down for too many problems. I learned how to rebuild proper digestion after mine shut down from the side effects of all the steroids, narcotics, and anti-inflammatory drugs. I was addicted to narcotics, muscle relaxers, and antidepressants. I couldn't work, I lost jobs. I went bankrupt. You name it, I did it. I overcame the physical, mental, emotional, spiritual, and financial trauma of pain and illness. My dream is that you will too and that you'll believe it is possible.

Even though I was overwhelmed and consumed by pain, a little whisper inside me told me this was not to be my lot in life. So I read, I learned, I tried new things. I listened to the doctors and then said, "Hmmm...Does it have to be this way?" I asked the questions that no one was willing to ask. I hope that after reading this book, you will hear the little whisper too.

I spent many years and thousands of dollars learning, studying, and knocking on every door until I got the answers, results, and success I wanted and dreamed of. At the time, I did it for me. Now years later, I know I did it for you too. As a nurse I watched so many people immobilized by pain. Being a sensitive empath, I felt their pain and it made me dig deeper to find the answer to my burning question. Once I asked the questions, the answers were revealed, but I had to ask first.

I have walked this walk. Unlike many doctors who treat pain and have no personal experience with it, I have lived it and found a way out. I have to admit it was not what I expected to find when I first went searching, but I met with success that baffled most of my doctors. I'm okay with that, and trust me, you will be too. Be willing to take a different path and you can get different results.

WHERE SHOULD YOU START?

Over the years, hundreds of clients and people I've met during public speaking events have thought that I had some sort of special or magical exception. They played *make believe* that their story was different or that they were worse off. They didn't believe that what I did was possible for them. But that is not true. I have been where they are.

For many, many years, patients suffered with symptoms of fibromyalgia and were told it was "all in their heads." Because it was mostly women who presented with symptoms, doctors dismissed the chronic pain and cluster of symptoms as psychosomatic, or *all in your head*. Once the medical industry has realized its prevalence in the last 20 years and that they could make a profit from it, they conveniently discovered a test to confirm a diagnosis of this often debilitating disease.

For some, just having a diagnosis from a doctor is such a relief that they're willing to stop there, to accept the diagnosis as their long-term fate and put up with *management* of their condition. If you are one of these people, grab a hold of yourself: *It doesn't have to be this way!*

The place to start is with new beliefs! Start with new beliefs about your body, about medicine, and about what is possible for you. I am going to encourage you to not have faith in a diagnosis. Doctors told me I wouldn't walk again. They were wrong. They told me that they couldn't help me. They told me, "I'm sorry, Martha, we've done everything we can. We've used everything that modern medicine has available to us." They had no answers for how I could return to my previous state of health. And they were right because the answer to my health was not up to them. It was between me and my beliefs. I had to find my own path.

This is not a matter of religious beliefs or convictions. Religion is religion. No matter what your religious beliefs are, the fact remains (and science has proven) that we are bundles of energy. It is in all of us. It is in me and it is in you. I have seen it and I have felt it. It is in everyone. Let me say it again: *You have a benevolent, energetic, healing life force inside you!* Start there. Choose to flip the switch. Choose to switch your beliefs. Choose who is really going to be in charge of your outcome and your health.

You can learn how to heal your current situation. You can choose to take 100 percent responsibility. This book will give you the tools that I used to do this.

HEALING AND CURING

Curing is the absence of a physical symptom in your body. The doctor says, "Mrs. Smith, you are cured. The chemotherapy worked. We don't see any signs of cancer in your body." The physical signs of illness are gone. But has healing occurred?

Healing is a state of complete wholeness and well-being. It is a dynamic state of balance among physical, mental, emotional, and spiritual health. We have numerous approaches and books that address the physical aspects of healing. I believe the missing components that have not been addressed and can produce long-lasting, tangible healing results are the mental, emotional ("stress-related"), and spiritual aspects that cause illness and pain. These are the significant aspects that I present in this book.

I have noticed that people who are willing to accept this and involve all of these aspects in their self-care routine are the ones who relieve their illness, completely and permanently.

This is the stipulation. You have to be willing to try new things, new approaches, and new systems. Be willing to clear out old ideas and beliefs. Be willing to take responsibility for your future. Be willing to do things that you have not done before. Don't leave it up to the doctors. Don't settle and don't continue to look for answers in a system that is for sick care, not health care. The definition of insanity: doing the same thing over and over and expecting to get different results.

When you begin to heal the spiritual and mental causes of illness, you will be able to alleviate the pain and symptoms in your physical body. But you must learn to use your mind and spirit in positive, life-affirming ways, not in the same ways to which you are accustomed.

Have you ever had this happen to you or someone you know? You think that you've healed some sort of ailment in your body, only to have a pain or symptom show up somewhere else shortly after? When the pain in your neck started to feel better, did you notice that your stomach started burning and you experienced frequent indigestion?

If we are willing to change the way we view common chronic health problems from a *big picture* perspective, as a spiritual opportunity, then we can find a new opening and the ability to do more than just manage them. We can send them away.

Part One of this book tells a narrative story of my journey through three back surgeries, fibromyalgia, living in a wheelchair, and how I made my way back to health and vitality, along with the spiritual lessons I learned. Part Two gives you the exercises and tools that helped me to reverse the fibromyalgia, pain, and symptoms. I tried *a lot* of things; some worked and some didn't. There were many things I did in the beginning that kept me stuck in a victim state and my own crap. That is the current problem I find with a lot of the holistic therapies and modalities—they still don't get at the *root cause*. In Part Two, I have given you the tools that empowered me to get to the core cause of my problems and remove them. So let's get started!

PART ONE

Starting the Journey and Crossing the Bridge

Natural forces within us are the true healers of disease. —

Hippocrates

CHAPTER ONE

Hindsight is Always 20/20

*You can start out with nothing, and out of nothing, and out of no way, a
way will be made.* —Rev. Michael Beckwith

N o matter when it comes, I am grateful for hindsight. Without it, I would not be able to share the insights that emerged from my 10-year journey out of struggle and pain. When my journey began, if anyone had told me I would be writing this story from the comfort of my home office while my employees were caring wholeheartedly for my business, I would have said that they had made a mistake, gotten the wrong person. Without the wisdom and guidance I received from Holy Spirit, I couldn't have seen the divinity in my pain. I couldn't have predicted how perfect and joy-full my life would become.

Over the last 20 years people have asked how I did it. How did I heal from three back surgeries and crippling pain? What I discovered through those years of trial and tribulation was that I was being led to my "remembrance." I have come to know that Holy Spirit will call each and every human being toward their own remembrance in its own unique way. It was my willingness to acknowledge and follow my "path of remembrance" that led to my complete healing and reversal of pain. Are you willing to move toward your remembrance? It is from this place that I begin my story.

There are many places in my story that make me feel vulnerable, of which I am not proud. There are places that even now still cause a twinge of guilt, shame, or fear in my belly. But my heart and soul are whole and complete, and it is from that wholeness that I am willing to share the bumped, torn, tattered, and dark places where I used to live. If you recognize any of these places within yourself, you will know how deep I had to dig within for my hope, inspiration, and remembrance, and perhaps you will be willing to dig deep for yours.

We're all going to pay a visit to the *dark side* at some point in our lives. The trick is to make a conscious choice not to stay there or live there. It is merely smoke and mirrors and not where the truth is. You must *choose* to only be a "visitor." It is clearly a choice, which I didn't know 30 years ago. I hadn't seen the path I was choosing. I invite you to observe from the "big picture" perspective with an open mind and an opportunity for spiritual growth.

From this perspective you can actually move directly *into* illness and pain, unravel its mystery, and make sense of its presence and purpose. Yes, I am going to ask you to move towards your pain, rather than away from it. When you do you will become part of a global and universal shift that is changing the face of medicine and healing. This shift will likely not complete itself in our lifetime, but based on what I have seen, it will happen.

I can't tell you where I first heard the phrase, "What you resist, persists," but I have come to be great friends with it. It created a significant awareness for me that would be the key to restoring health. The current remedies of nerve blocks, anti-inflammatory and prescription narcotic drugs help patients to resist the *cause* of pain. *They seek to numb us from the reality of our bodies.* When we learn to move towards the pain we break our personal pattern of resistance, allowing for healing and reversal of illness.

I wholeheartedly believe that if you're willing to move *towards* your pain or illness, you will uncover your happy, healthy body. You will find *your* remembrance. (Hint: your purpose has never been and never will be to struggle, be on disability, handicapped, or living with severe chronic pain).

I know that I took the long way back to my remembrance, albeit to gather knowledge, wisdom, and information to help others. I spent several years gathering pieces of wisdom and healing through trial and error. I have since learned that it doesn't have to be so hard and take so long. Clients I've worked with in my private practice who have applied the tools and principles I explain here have had much quicker results than I did. Those who have been willing to examine new spiritual concepts and look at old worn-out beliefs have met with lasting success.

It is not just the idea of holistic care that creates success; there are many holistic practitioners who don't ever lead their patients to health and well-being. The holistic healing community often keeps their clients dis-empowered, keeping them "coming back for more," rather than teaching and empowering clients by giving them the tools they need to heal. My desire is to teach you how to be your own healer.

HOW DID I GET HERE?

Wanting to be someone else is a waste of the person you are. — Kurt Cobain

It may seem odd, but I honestly can't remember most of my childhood except for bits and pieces here and there. I've seen lots of family pictures that indicate I appeared to be happy. My dad used to tell me stories of what a happy, carefree, adventurous little girl I was. I remember snippets of second grade, third grade, and junior high, but overall there are many years of my childhood that are still blank to this day.

I hear others account stories of their family, siblings, memories, vacations, and holidays, and I just don't seem to remember most of those things. I don't remember being particularly happy or unhappy. If I had to guess, I would say I felt happy in my younger years from age four to ten or eleven. Perhaps it was in the awkward years of adolescence and puberty when it became fuzzy and I blocked most of it out in an effort to cope with peer pressure, trauma, and change.

I know from the rearview mirror that this is as significant as any part of my story. I would come to realize that these were years that I created beliefs about life and reality that would set me up to live with chronic pain in my body. I can tell you that what I thought were unique circumstances only to me were in fact part of the three universal fears unraveling in my life. As a spiritual student and teacher, it is clear to me that every person will come to experience and deal with these three universal fears throughout their lives; they are, after all, universal. The three universal fears are fear of abandonment or being alone, fear of being unworthy (low self-esteem), and fear of danger and insecurity (the essential question being—Is the world a safe and friendly place where I trust and believe in goodness?).

It seemed to me that I just woke up one day in high school lost and confused, not like a typical lost teenager, but as if I had not been present for the first 15 years of my life. I had no real direction in my mind or heart except to pour myself into figure skating and sports. I had been skating since I was five years old and competed at the local level. I spent a lot of time before and after school skating or in team sports. It kept me busy. My mother had decided that keeping me busy would cure my melancholy of misdirection.

My early school testing ranked me well above average in reading and writing, but I struggled with math. Doing something creative would have suited me just fine, but I had no real inklings or passion for what that might be. I was always envious of the students in high school who had a clear idea of exactly what they wanted to do with their lives. Some left high school knowing that they wanted to be doctors, or own a dance studio. I liked painting and writing. My mother's opinion on those crafts as a chosen career was—"I didn't spend all that money on private schools for you to become a "starving artist." I thought maybe I could join the Ice Capades for a few years. Travel, adventure, and being on tour sounded fun, but being raised in a good German family meant that fun wasn't an acceptable career goal. Talk of the Ice Capades pushed my mother right over the edge.

Before I knew it, I was packed into the back of the family station wagon on my way to a private girl's junior college 96 miles south of Kansas City. I guess my mom figured that getting me away from negative influences and boys would somehow change everything, as if the boys and negative influences wouldn't find me in Missouri. I think I had about a 1.1 GPA at the end of my first semester. I tried to be honest with myself—I just wasn't *into* it. I had the idea that I would study nutrition and food science, but the curriculum had way too many math and science classes (funny how I would later breeze through those classes in nursing school). So I opted to take a second look at journalism. I thought to myself—Yeah, that's it, journalism, I'll pick that. Like a spin of the wheel, I'll pick that. I told myself it really didn't make any difference what I chose for the first two years. I could take the core curriculum classes that were necessary for all majors. At the same time, however, I felt tremendous external pressure to *have a direction*. I began to critically judge myself and put myself down because I had no burning desire for what I wanted to do with my life.

Looking back, my very first career inclinations became the things I most love now (Whoa! There it is: *what we resist, persists*. Note to self: Pay attention to your inner urgings). My earliest passions and inclinations never went away. They tugged at me until it became too difficult to ignore, you might even say, too pain-full to ignore. Is it possible that we experience physical pain as a divine message that we have strayed from or ignored our true path? I believe so.

My early interests became part of my career and livelihood, but not in a conventional way. In my own creative way I learned to use my gifts to serve a greater good, along with a big push from God.

It took me many years to understand what was really going on. I see hundreds of clients in my business every year who are looking for validation of their unique talents and gifts. We still live in a cultural environment that rewards more right brain, Type A careers over those that are "feminine" and spiritual in nature. It is easy to see this validated by the salaries of professions that were once dominated by woman, like teaching and nursing. When I was young there was a lot of pressure to conform, to become a high achiever in a high-earning, highly respected career. I was not encouraged to be creative. Our government and school systems are proliferating this model today with their *testing* model as the standard to fit in and be ranked. If students don't "make the mark" in this model, they are considered underperformers and underachievers. There is no room for individuality or creativity. The average parent is brainwashed to raise children who "measure up" or excel in order to fit in and to create self-esteem, value, and worth.

Let me take just a moment here to expand on the idea of trusting God and trusting your path and inner urgings, and to elaborate on how that relates to pain and illness. Although I am grateful for my lessons, I could have avoided so much suffering if I had been encouraged to flourish in my passions and intuition, if I'd had the inner strength and courage to follow what I felt in my heart. At the time, though, I felt so much pressure to obey my mother and her controlling dictates. Our parents mean well, they really do. But unless they are highly "enlightened" (and most were not back in those days in the 1970s), they can unknowingly project their unfulfilled wishes and desires onto their children, wanting them to be, do, and have everything that they did not. This one factor alone is the cause of so much pain and illness, holding and storing guilt and shame that we are a disappointment to our parents or someone else in our lives or family.

I see so many clients who are withering away inside, enveloped by pain, and too fearful to trust themselves and their natural inclinations. Their hearts are begging them to take a chance on their dreams and visions. God is doing everything he can to get their attention. Fearful *gut* emotions hold incredibly powerful energy, strong enough to cause chronic and debilitating pain and illness.

Unable to listen fully or act upon my own desires, I found myself at college in the Midwest, away from home for the first time. Being footloose and free, it wasn't long before I found myself in a reckless downward spiral. I still felt lost and had no prospects for a job in journalism even though I finished my two years at the junior college. Having lost most of my self-esteem and not having the courage to stand up for myself and what I really wanted, I began to float through life in any direction that was in front of me. I still had no real direction at the end of my first two years of college so I moved to Arkansas with my boyfriend where he attended college.

And so my life would go on in this way for the next several years. It seemed like I moved in whatever direction the wind was blowing, waiting and hoping for something or someone outside myself to give me a direction, a plan. I finished college in Arkansas. I got a degree in interior design and started pursuing artistic and creative talents. I got a job at a furniture store as an in-house designer. Away from my boyfriend and now in a town two hours away, I would drink and party with colleagues in the evening, trying to fill the emptiness and void. Life just kept on moving and I became more and more addicted to the partying life. I smoked cigarettes and pot, drank alcohol nearly every day, and eventually began to use cocaine on a regular basis. I spent most of my work day waiting for the evenings to arrive. I made pretty good money but I spent most of it on partying. After three years of this addicted lifestyle, I was even more depressed and lost.

Ten years after I left the house that I grew up in, I would return, exhausted, depleted, lost, and empty inside. There was a particular thought that kept ruminating in my mind and heart, over and over again: How did I get here? Why am I not married, with two kids, a dog, and a white picket fence? How did my life turn out this way?

It seemed that the one thing I had accomplished in my ten years after graduating from high school was that I catered to the restlessness deep within myself. I had tried recreational drugs, alcohol, endless first dates, and just about everything I could think of to escape and avoid searching within for answers. I had run out of rope. I hadn't managed to hang myself yet, so I guessed I would have to settle down and figure out why I felt so lost. My low self-worth had caused me to focus on filling the emptiness I felt from external sources. The deep emotional pain within was never soothed by these external trappings. Tired and nearly broke, I moved back into my parents' house to regroup. I didn't know it at the time, but from that day forward I had periods of surrender to a *higher power* and Holy Spirit took over the direction of my life and purpose.

I certainly experienced long periods of resistance, but I had allowed the divine to enter my consciousness and take direction of my future. Mind you, I was still in the driver's seat with my hands on the steering wheel, but from time to time I let God be my co-pilot. Eventually I was willing to let him do the steering while I read the map. I had done things *my way* and all that had gotten me was lost and empty. One night in desperation I came to beg God for help. My pleading went something like this: Please show me a way, tell me what to do, help me find my place in this world, or take me, put me out of my misery.

Back in those days, like everything I had searched for, I saw "God" as something outside myself. He was a white-bearded man in a humble but gorgeous and glorious robe, with a big gold "G" around his neck. He had been judging my behavior and deemed me sinful and unfit, unworthy of "the good life." With nowhere else to turn, I figured *he* was the only one with the answers to help me.

I couldn't have been more wrong about the nature of *who* I considered my creator to be. I ask you—Have you, or anyone you know, seen this *man* that has been portrayed and projected as "God"? Have you seen the *who*? This man in the robe?

Let me clarify here my use of the words *God*, *Spirit*, *Holy Spirit*, *Universe*, and *Creator* before moving forward. The word *God* is a term that has created wars, turmoil, fear, massacres, and death. That is not what I believe our creator would intend for itself in its name.

I believe that you and I were created from *life eternal*, a benevolent, everlasting consciousness of love and energy—a "what," not a "who." This energy exists in everyone and everything in the universe. From this I came, and to this I will return. I believe that the *life everlasting* to which religious text and scriptures refer is the energy of the Holy Spirit and it is present for all of us, as all of us, in all of us, surrounding all of us. It is the universe and the universe is it.

Think about it: How do we get the miracle of a little human being growing inside another human being from the comingling of a sperm and an egg!? There are life forces at work here that are really incomprehensible. We are bundles of miraculous energy.

Once in the physical body (at birth), I believe this energy and life force expresses itself as what I call *the higher self*, or *soul*. It is this soul and higher self, the spirit of this energy, which animates the body and will return back to itself as life everlasting.

This spirit is pure love. It does not create war, it does not create evil, and it does not create illness, pain, or death. Its nature is to express itself, as itself, pure love and light. Personally, when I use the word *God* I am able to see, feel, and embody this perspective, but I do understand that for many this is not the case. For many the word *God* is associated with religion, churches, wars, right, wrong, good, bad, sin, repentance, something to prove, and the issue of whose God is right—Whose God is the best? Which is the right one to worship? This is not *my* "God."

When I use the word *God* in this book, I am referring to the divine spirit of love and eternal life and goodness, creating as itself, from itself, and returning always to itself, Love. From here on, you will see me use the words *God, Spirit, Universe, Love,* and *Creator* interchangeably. For me they are all the same. They all refer to what I have come to know and embody within myself as God. The *All one*, the *At-one-ment.* All God, all love, all divine creation, all goodness.

When I look at all the goodness that is expressed in the world through this eternal spirit, the order and benevolence I see—the moon, the sun, the stars, the oceans, the tide, the birds, the bees, the flowers, the seasons, I see and feel the love. It is the intangible, unexplainable, yet palpable and real energy that creates an entire fruit-bearing apple tree from a few tiny seeds. I see the love and energy that animates the seeds, soil, water, and sunlight to bear fruit…over and over again. To my knowledge, no one has waged war over this eternal loving energy. No one has died for this. When I use the word *God* I know it as this benevolent life force that wants nothing more than for us to express its fullness and glory, right here, right now, as *heaven on earth.* If any of these terms cause discomfort for you, I ask that you suspend judgment on my language and substitute whatever words work best for you, so long as you feel peace with the words you choose. I am not here to argue about terms, but to acknowledge a holy, divine spirit.

As I surrendered to God that day, with my begging prayer, it was not without confusion and struggle. I allowed Spirit to work through me, healing, shaping, and directing me to my purpose and healing, yet it was years before I would fully surrender and accept the truth.

Okay, I get it. If you're like I was, living with chronic illness or pain, right about now you're thinking, "What does any of this have to do with me? What does this have to do with what I'm experiencing?" I'm going to ask you to look at the belief systems and old paradigms that have gotten stuck in our minds, our bodies, and our health care (sick care) system. I'm asking you to be open to learning about the spiritual and meta-physical (*meta* meaning beyond physical) approaches to healing illness and pain.

This is a new opportunity, not readily mentioned or offered to you or others who are living with chronic pain (or any other illness for that matter). It is an opportunity to accept a new path to become your own best healer as I learned to do, so bear with me.

On that one fateful day as I desperately spoke to God, I had a light bulb moment. In my head I believed that my life really sucked, but in my heart I didn't blame God. I remember thinking—if the worst God gave me is less than perfect vision, I'm pretty lucky. I didn't want to continue to waste my life and energy partying and escaping from the restless angst I felt inside. I wanted to leave some kind of good in the world. I decided to go to nursing school, and something about that career choice felt different from the previous ones.

That choice started moving me in the direction of my purpose. Nursing school was just the first step in Spirit leading me to my life of health, healing, and service. So in 1987 I started my clinical studies in a two-year program at a local community college, and that summer I got a part-time job as a nurse's aide at a nursing home. I had moved back into my parents' house. It was less than ideal after living on my own for ten years, but it made the most sense financially to be able to study full-time and without having to worry about working full-time to pay bills.

There I was, 28 years old and living with Mom and Dad. Their marriage was strained, at best, and had been for many years. Eventually, I would be cast in the middle of their emotionally distressing divorce. During the next few years, any time I saw my mother I was afraid of her because of her underlying fears expressed as rage and emotional instability. I was riding on a wacky roller coaster every time I was near her, being tossed about in all different directions by her unstable and sometimes irrationally violent behavior.

In the midst of her battles with my father, she came to me one day, pleading. She walked up very close to me, about six inches away from my face. My heart pounded faster and harder with each step she took. With a clenched, tight jaw, she looked at me square in the eyes with pure fear and desperation. She said, "Please tell your father not to do this. It's financial suicide. He'll listen to you."

There it was out in the open. A pivotal moment and lesson in my life, she had unleashed from deep within herself one of the three universal fears. She had unleashed the fear that had been the negative driving energy in her life and marriage. It was an irrational fear that her mother had taught her and a belief that had been ingrained and programmed into my beliefs and my cells since I was a child. How could I have missed it all these years?

In that moment I realized that this was how I learned not to trust *life*. She had taught me not to trust myself. She had taught me that I shouldn't trust life to provide all my needs. She had taught me to be fearful of life, expecting disaster at any turn. I had come to believe that I was always just a moment away from disaster and ruin. Where had she learned this? How had this been her reality? She had never wanted for anything that I could see. We lived in a very nice house, I went to private schools, and we belonged to country clubs. Both of my grandparents owned businesses and were considered successful. My grandparents had paid for my mother and father to get a college education. They had never been in any financial hardship that I could see. Why was she so afraid?

Once I realized that she wasn't in a violent mood, I took a deep breath and said, "You'll have to talk to Dad about your situation," and I walked away.

What I pondered for the next few days was the idea of what she hadn't said, "Tell your father not to do this. I love him!" I thought to myself of the times in relationships when I felt bad for something I had said or done, and would apologize by saying, "I'm sorry, I love you." Where was her apology of love?

I will never forget the feeling of fear and desperation that came out of her. They say the eyes are the window to the soul. How could a soul be filled with so much fear, panic, and desperation? I would come to realize that the fear she held deep within her body was not the nature of her soul. I was not seeing her soul reflecting out at me that day, but human suffering created by the mind. I would come to know that as a child, I had felt that very same energy coming from her and had unknowingly absorbed it into the cells of my body.

For the next few days it was as if a full-length feature film was playing in my mind's eye. I remembered miscellaneous scenes and scenarios from my life strung together as a theme, only now they had relevance and wisdom attached to them. I was able to deconstruct the fragments that had been subconsciously engrained in me. I remembered an argument when she said to me, "This is the thanks I get? I sent you to private schools so that you could meet someone who would be able to 'take care of you,' someone from 'a good family.'" She went on to say, "With your expensive tastes, you better marry a doctor or a lawyer, otherwise you will be a very unhappy girl." At 20 years old, she thought of me as a "girl," not a young woman. I imagined that she was repeating the very same sentiment that her mother had said to her.

I would come to realize how those words and beliefs set me up for the chronic pain that I held in my body as fibromyalgia, sciatica, and back pain. This was a clear demonstration of a mantra that I would become very familiar with: "the issues are in the tissues." It is a concept in the forefront of spiritual and metaphysical healing, the idea that we can store emotional issues in our body that can cause illness and pain. It's what modern medicine would call stress-related illness. Stress is really nothing more than unresolved emotional issues that we hold in our tissues.

With this realization, I grew angry. I picked sides in my parents' ugly and bitter divorce battle. My father had been nothing but encouraging and supportive of my choices and decisions since I had moved back home. He did everything in his power to create an environment that would support me moving forward in my career as a nurse.

My mother, on the other hand, had been critical, judgmental, controlling, and manipulative for a great portion of my life, and it was only getting worse since moving back home. Instead of releasing her dysfunctional fears toward my father, which she had been doing for the last ten years, she now had someone new to whom she could send the negative energy. She directed her fear towards me.

It became crystal clear that the further away I could get from her, the better off I would be. I wanted to heal what was behind these realizations and move past them. Needless to say, I was not endowed with high self-worth or esteem growing up in this energy and environment. No wonder I was lost. I had no sense of value or worth. How was I to trust life if I wasn't able to trust myself?

I can imagine you might be saying to yourself, "I didn't have any of these conditions in my life. No one in my family had these sorts of fears or issues when I was growing up. This couldn't possibly be the source of my pain. This couldn't possibly have anything to do with why I have arthritis, or migraines, or sciatica, or fibromyalgia. I had a normal family. I had a normal childhood. I was never lost or confused." Maybe that's true, maybe it isn't. We have a great ability to repress our discomforts.

Our body and mind are protected by the ego. The ego will do anything to protect itself, including repressing and suppressing emotions and feelings that are too painful for us to process or handle. It is this process of protection that allows us to store, albeit mostly unconsciously, our emotional issues and discomforts in the tissues of our cells and organs. It is in our tissues that we can store memories that lay dormant for years until we are forced to deal with them. It is when they come up from the depths of repression that we may experience them as pain. They are no longer buried where they can't hurt us. Now they are felt not as emotional pain but experienced as physical pain in the body. In our current health care system, most go to a doctor for answers when these issues arise. Doctors do everything in their power to annihilate the symptoms, and in this place we miss all opportunity to be healed.

It is in this place that our system for healing and reversing pain has fallen apart. There isn't a pill or procedure anywhere in medicine that can *heal* emotional pain. We may be able to divert the emotional pain or "block" our experience of feeling it, but the memory of it is still trapped in the body. The painful emotions are still in the tissues.

A perfect example of this is the feeling of grief that one experiences after losing a loved one. Ask anyone who has been through this kind of emotional loss and they'll tell you there's nothing you can do to avoid the feeling of grief. It is real. It is tangible. It is a physical feeling. Even though we most commonly call grief an "emotion," it is felt in our hearts, our chest, and our body. There is no pill that heals it. There are medications to help you sleep and get through the days of depression surrounding the loss of a loved one, but only by facing the loss and the feeling of the emotions in our physical body can we get through it to the other side. Some do, and some don't.

And so it is with pain. If we don't acknowledge the truth about what chronic pain really is, we don't have the opportunity to heal it. I ask you to keep this in mind and be willing to explore this if you are living with chronic pain. Chances are very likely that this area of your body is congested with the energy of a repressed feeling or emotion. I can almost guarantee it.

So there I was in the midst of this family turmoil back in 1987. It was between my first and second semesters of nursing school that I got a part-time summer job as a nurse's aide in a nursing home in order to gain experience working in my new chosen profession. It was a hot summer July evening forever etched in my memory—July 7, 1987. We were short-staffed with only three nurse's aides to care for 40 patients. The temperature and atmosphere on the unit was hot, humid, and unbearable for both the staff and the frail elderly. In those days they still allowed patients to be physically restrained in wheelchairs, tied up, literally, and strapped to a chair. Imagine what that does to one's spirit and emotions. It makes them restless and combative.

I was just about at the end of my rope that day. Things had escalated the night before between my mother and father. I had come home from work to find the "good china" smashed all over the floor in the kitchen and family room. There was an eerie sense of quiet in the house. I wondered what I would find as I walked up the stairs to my bedroom that night. Thoughts raced through my mind and made my heart race with fear. Being raised to expect the worst case scenario I imagined, What if they had killed each other in a rage? What was I going to find at the top of the stairs? Based on what I had seen in the kitchen, it seemed completely reasonable. The house was dark except for one small light on in the kitchen. I was so scared. I didn't want to look. I didn't want to know. I hoped everyone was in their own rooms sleeping.

I walked up the stairs with my heart pounding out of my chest. As I reached the top step a voice called out. My father was alive.

"Martha?" he called out.

"Dad? Are you okay?"

"Yes, I'm fine!" he answered.

"Where's Mother?" I asked. "What happened downstairs, Dad?" I walked into my father's bedroom to talk.

"She had a fitful rage and started throwing and smashing things," my father explained.

Suddenly, I looked to see a light turn on in the other bedroom. My mother crept into the doorway with smoke and fire still coming out of her. There was no discussion. I was physically and emotionally exhausted. I went to my room and locked the door. I tried to sleep but I was mostly just frightened and couldn't wait for the sun to come up. Things would feel safer in the light of day. There was no discussion of the incident the next day. Everyone went about their day like the night before had never happened. That's how my parents dealt with things. Anything that was difficult got swept under the proverbial rug. I never felt comfortable in those situations, knowing that we had laid a minefield of bombs underneath that rug over the years that could ignite without warning at any moment.

When I got to work that next afternoon, the anxiety and distress on the unit was palpable. Maybe it was because I hadn't slept the night before. Maybe it was my state of exhaustion from continuous stress, but everyone at the nursing home that next evening seemed out of sorts. The staff was out of sync. It was beastly hot. A resident who we fondly called "Harry Houdini" because of his frequent attempts to make sensational escapes from his wheelchair was assigned to my care. He was restrained with a "posey vest," a type of medical restraint used to confine a patient to a bed or chair for their own safety. The vest is placed on the patient and mesh straps are tied either to each side of the bed or together to the back of a wheelchair. They were used to prevent patients from injuring themselves by falling or climbing out of the bed or chair. This patient, however, spent the entire evening trying to untie the straps so that he could get up from his chair. Never underestimate the will and cunning of an elderly patient who wants to be set free!

In the midst of fatigue, dehydration, and being short-staffed, two other aides and I made our very best efforts to give our full attention and best care to the residents on our unit. Our charge nurse did her very best to sit on her butt at the nurses' station, sipping large tumblers of iced tea and pretending to do charting documentation and organizing the medication cart.

Every time I tried tending to feeding, bathing, and toileting my patients, "Harry Houdini" screamed "Help!" at the top of his lungs while trying to untie himself from the vest restraint. He was desperately and consistently trying to get out of his wheelchair. I had to stop what I was doing, rush to him for his safety, and spend the next ten minutes trying to sweet talk and coerce him to let me retie the straps. He was not able to walk. If he tried to get up, he would hurt himself. He was so focused on being restrained and breaking free from his restraint that I don't think he could remember that he couldn't walk.

This went on for several hours until we could finally put him to bed. I was exhausted and drained. I asked the charge nurse several times for help, to no avail. She said she was too busy. I begged her to let him sit up at the desk with her while she did her work in the hopes that it would distract him. She refused to help. Finally, after five hours of this dynamic, things calmed down a bit and I asked my charge nurse if I could take a quick break. She said that I could after I answered the call light down the hall. I told her I felt like I was going to pass out from heat stroke. She was not concerned. She said, "After you answer Mrs. Gray's bathroom call light and get her off the toilet, you can go on a break. You can't just go on a break and leave her sitting on the toilet."

I made a conscious decision about my nursing career in that moment. When I became a nurse I would NEVER treat another human being the way she was treating me. She was a disgrace to the nursing profession. How had she become so callous and uncaring? I would never, could never, be so uncaring and oblivious to the human condition. I would treat my staff and my aides well and equally. I would always pitch in to share the load for the well-being of everyone.

I went down to Mrs. Gray's room and entered her bathroom. I pulled the cord on the wall to turn off the red blinking light and attempted to get her off the toilet. She had suffered a stroke and needed help with most activities. She could stand and hold on to the handicap bars attached to the wall for a short amount of time. She was morbidly obese, weighing somewhere around 325 pounds and five feet, four inches tall. It was always the same routine at bed time with her. We had done this many times before. We would count together, "1, 2, 3, up we go." She would pull herself up, holding onto the metal bars while I boosted her up, pulled her pants up, and then pivoted her back into her wheelchair.

I had been trained on how to properly lift residents, even those who were overweight. Mrs. Gray had to be washed up when I went to get her off the toilet. Her buttocks and legs weren't clean. I guess the fact that it was so hot and humid contributed to the devastating chain of events that would happen next.

We got her up to standing and she held on with both hands to the bar while I washed her up, but her skin was moist and sticky with sweat from the heat and humidity. I usually only had to pull on her cotton underpants and set her in the wheelchair. Then I could put her nightie over her head while she was sitting down. But on this night she insisted that she would stay up for a while and did not want to put her nightie on. It was her right, and I always strived to give residents as much freedom as possible. This was, after all, their home. I honored her request and bent down to pull her pants up. It was hot! She was sweating profusely. I went from front to back to side to side to front, trying to inch her way-too-tight polyester pants up her sweaty, sticky legs and buttocks. It was taking forever as they got bunched up and stuck in place. I lost good body mechanics. I was hot and exhausted.

She began to cry and scream, "Hurry, I can't hold on! I'm going to fall."

"No, Mrs. Gray, you'll be fine," I said. "Just one more second. Hang on...almost there..."

She started to let go of the bars. I reached over. I reached around. I bent over...Snap! I couldn't move. I was nearly frozen in place with pain shooting through my back like a strike of lightning. I can still remember it today as vivid as that day. She cried louder. She was frightened. I was too exhausted to be frightened.

I was a rookie. In hindsight, there are so many things that I would have done differently that night. But it was too late. It was not meant to be. I could not reverse what happened.

Despite my exhaustion, all I could think about was the safety and well-being of my patient. We were both scared. I didn't want to disappoint her. I wanted her to feel safe. I didn't want her to fall. I didn't want her to get hurt. I didn't want to lose her trust. I put my arms and all my strength around her and held her up. I let her pants stay where they were.

I pulled the emergency chain and called out for help, and waited there with her in my arms until help arrived. Thank God my fellow aides were on my side. Somehow they knew and came quickly, but the damage had been done. I could hardly move. It took me about four minutes to be able to stand up straight and another few minutes to walk out of the room and down the hall. I told one of the aides what had just happened but never let on to Mrs. Gray that I had just hurt myself. The other two aides cursed a few words under their breath about the charge nurse and said that they would finish up with Mrs. Gray and that I should get some ice on my back. I went on my break.

All the while the charge nurse was still sitting at the desk. I said nothing and walked out the back door to get some air. I took six Motrin tabs, thinking they would make everything right.

I returned to the building twenty minutes later. There was only ninety minutes left on my shift. I can make it, I told myself. I'll be okay. I am not a quitter. I'm strong. I can get through this. I'll be okay.

As I hobbled gingerly down the hall to tend to the rest of my patients, I went in to apologize to Mrs. Gray. She was now in bed. Apparently the ordeal tuckered her out. So much for staying up for a while. She apologized to me. She may not have had control of her body, but she had perfect control of her mind and she felt awful about the situation. She told me, "You'll make a really good nurse, Martha." We both comforted and reassured each other and shared a moment. That was the last time I would ever see Mrs. Gray.

As I walked down the hall to tend to the rest of my patients, Charge Nurse "Ratchet" came out of the second to last room at the far end of the hall. She had fire in her eyes. She yelled my name and ordered me into the resident's room. She had walked in to give him his evening medications and found him in the same position that he was in two hours earlier. Unable to move or position himself, it was my responsibility to turn and position him every two hours.

In front of the patient she demanded, "Why have you not turned this man in the last two hours?" I looked up at her in complete disbelief! Had she been completely oblivious to the chaos that had been going on that evening on the unit? Did she not see the signs of pain all over my face? Did she not see how I was holding my body, barely able to stand, let alone walk? Did she not see the sweat and tears running down my brow into the corners of my eyes?

I could hardly speak from disbelief. I slowly muttered, "Because Harry Houdini was untying himself from his chair all night, Mrs. Gray nearly fell on the bathroom floor, and I think I seriously hurt my back!"

Without a moment of hesitation she exclaimed, "I am not concerned about your physical condition. You are supposed to turn him every two hours. Look at him, he's going to get bedsores. You're lucky I don't write you up. When I'm finished with his meds, you can turn him."

I said nothing. I stood there in shock and disbelief. My mouth couldn't even create any response. I waited for her to leave the room. I collapsed on the floor in a silent whimper the moment she left the room. It would take me fifteen minutes to pull myself together before I could leave the room. The resident in that room was near death and mostly unconscious. He was unaware that I was crying in the corner of his room. I walked down to the nurses' station, completed my documentation, and told the nurse I was leaving. I didn't care what she did; she was welcome to write me up. I would be filing a complaint with management first thing in the morning. I left thirty minutes before my shift was over and could hardly sit in my car to make it the five-mile drive home. I never returned to work there. That evening was the "straw" that broke my back, literally.

Things were calm at my parents' house when I returned home that night. I went straight to bed with an ice pack on my back. I figured a good night's rest would heal whatever had happened to me while I was caring for Mrs. Gray. I was wrong.

The next morning I woke up, put my feet on the floor, and could barely stand. When I tried to straighten up my back quivered with pain. I made my way downstairs to the kitchen. What would I find this morning on the home front? No matter what it was, it would pale in comparison to the pain I was feeling in my back and buttocks. Once again in complete resistance to life, I asked myself, "How did I get here?"

CHAPTER TWO

The Straw That Broke My Back

If we really love ourselves, everything in our life works. —Louise Hay

L ittle did I know with the start of that next morning that it was the beginning of my ten-year battle against daily chronic pain.

What was it that caused me to injure my back the night before while tending to Mrs. Gray? I was young, 28 years old. Women that age don't have "bad backs." I hadn't been in the nursing profession long enough to have weakened an otherwise strong and athletic body. I had been a competitive figure skater. I was muscular. That one little incidence of having to lean forward to support Mrs. Gray couldn't have caused this. And what was "this", this excruciating pain? I could understand and give into a pulled muscle or something, but from everything I had learned in my anatomy and physiology classes, the body is pretty intelligent and strong. After a week of doctors' appointments, testing, and chiropractors, I had a diagnosis: L4 bulging herniated disc.

I have come to realize that all of these events were divinely intertwined to lead me down a certain path in the direction of my highest good and purpose, but it would take me through some excruciatingly painful places before I would understand it all. Until I began to look at things from a spiritual perspective, I would not understand the significance of the events that unfolded over the next ten years and beyond.

A hidden blessing of significance on my healing journey was the fact that my injury at the nursing home that night thrust me into the workers' compensation system to seek medical care for the next 15 months. I couldn't have realized that what appeared to be a "slap in the face" from a government system that was supposed to support patients injured while working could become a lifelong blessing in disguise! When I was injured at the nursing home I was working part-time as a nurse's aide. My minimum wage pay was about 90 dollars a week. For the rest of my life, if I became disabled and unable to work because of this injury, New York State would pay me 65 dollars a week. I couldn't believe it. *It didn't pay for me to be hurt.* I was *highly* motivated to do whatever I could to get better.

That was a gift from God! I wasn't meant to be sitting around feeling sorry for myself. Spirit had different plans for me, but I didn't know it then. I couldn't see the spiritual advantage of being forced to get back to work. I can tell you without a doubt that it was the best thing that could have happened to me. Had I been offered any reasonable amount of money, I might have become like millions of Americans waiting for a broken down workers' compensation system to dictate the future of life, my earnings, and my health. I am deeply grateful that wasn't the case for me.

I could have just sat back, taken it easy, taken the narcotics, and never sought a way out of my situation. I could have let the doctors and the government tell me how my life and health were going to turn out. Things within this system never ran smoothly. It was a constant battle and struggle and the attorneys who were hired to represent me were lackadaisical and incompetent. They got paid by the system no matter the outcome. They had no skin in the game, no reason to fight for *me*.

Millions of patients fall victim to this environment, battling with workers' compensation for health care and wages. The best thing you can do is take your health into your own hands and become empowered. So many patients are enticed into believing that this is a system meant to help patients for the rest of their lives. It is not!

From a financial perspective, the sooner a patient comes to understand that this system is not in place to help them for the *long term*, the better chance a patient has of taking control of their future and their happiness. From a health perspective, it can cover some of the costs of health care, but there are many disadvantages to relying on this system for the best possible outcome. From a spiritual perspective, it is complete disaster to rely on this system. I am grateful that it ultimately paid for my resulting surgeries and medical care, but it is not a system that empowers patients, as you will learn in the following chapters.

During the next 15 months, I would seek out numerous medical doctors, chiropractors, physical therapists, and even acupuncturists, all to no avail. I began to take low doses of Darvocet every day just to be able to get through the day. In the fall I continued with my studies in nursing school, but it became increasingly difficult to sit in class or lift and move patients during my clinical rotations.

I found a job as a medical assistant working for a doctor in a large group practice. I moved out of my parents' house to live in an apartment and my dad moved out of the house that his father had built to get away from my mother and begin divorce proceedings. The next several years would be filled with emotional turmoil for him, and I was often stuck in the middle of their battles. Divorce is a difficult situation for a daughter, even as a young adult. Being 29 years old did not make it easier than it would have been if it happened when I was a young child.

In the winter semester I was only able to take a few of my core curriculum classes and one nursing lecture class. I was physically unable to continue at my previous level of activity. I was required to submit a formal appeal to the director of the nursing program to be able to separate my clinical and nursing theory classes. Working full-time and going to school full-time proved to be too much for me to handle. My back pain and sciatica increased and I began taking valium as a muscle relaxer and 800 milligrams of Motrin every six hours to reduce inflammation, and I had ditched my Darvocet for the stronger Vicodin prescription.

I continued like this until the end of my fall semester in December 1988, when it became nearly impossible to function. My grades were failing and everyone in my life had concerns for my current and future well-being. My professors were ready to kick me out of the nursing program. My boss invited me to go on an "extended leave" until I got better. I had foot drop and walked like an 80-year-old lady. I was determined to get my degree and nursing license; it was the key to a happy career and future. Like Steve Martin in the movie *The Jerk*, I would be *Somebody*. I would help others. I would be respected. I would have a *real job*.

It would have been a lot easier and better for my health if I didn't have to work full-time while going to school, but there just didn't seem to be any other way. I couldn't live on 65 dollars a week from workers' comp. I wasn't going to give up on nursing school. I worried all the time. But I reasoned with myself and God (the man in the robe)—if I could just get through and finish school, I'd be okay. I could slow down this crazy pace and I would make more money as a nurse.

Why was all this so important to me? Why was I putting so much pressure on my career to validate me as a human being, to make me feel valued and worthy? Who was this person? I had gone from playing and escaping with alcohol and recreational drugs to medicating with prescription drugs. I was anxious and depressed at the same time. I struggled financially to make ends meet. I worked and studied day and night. I pushed myself until I couldn't think or stand up.

It wasn't until many years later that I came to realize that my return back home was no mistake. God Spirit had a hand in that. I know now that Spirit loved me so much to put me in this situation so that I could resolve my emotions and move forward into my good, happy, healthy, and prosperous life. But it sure was covered with a lot of smoke and mirrors. God truly does work in mysterious ways.

Returning home became an opportunity to get thrown smack in the middle of all the old family and ancestral wounds so that they could be healed. Indeed, my issues were buried in my tissues, but first I would have to reach my dark night of the soul. Wasn't I already there? It certainly seemed so.

After fifteen months of living on prescription drugs and exhausting every medical intervention, I would have my first back surgery in January 1989. I went into the hospital early in the morning as an outpatient and went home that afternoon. The neurosurgeon performed what was then considered a new state-of-the-art back surgery called a percutaneous automated discectomy. While under general anesthesia, the doctor inserted a needle with a scope in through my hip to extract the damaged part of the disc from my body.

They claimed it was less invasive and had a quicker recovery time than making a large incision in my back. However, it was still back surgery. I went back to work at my job in the doctor's office a week later. Once again, I pushed myself. I had to get back to work. I needed the money. My boss was shocked that I was returning to work so quickly, but the doctors cleared me to return to work for "light duty"—no lifting. My boss approved.

Although I was improved enough to return to work, I was not able to start my last semester of clinical nursing rotation. They wouldn't give me clearance to return. There was too much risk and liability in allowing me to care for patients in the hospital. If there was an emergency that occurred, I might not be able to physically respond appropriately without injuring myself or compromising patient care. I would have to wait until the following semester.

I was able to take a few of my core curriculum classes, but not my clinical classes. I felt deeply discouraged. My path to financial freedom was on hold. It wouldn't be until the fall semester, September 1989, when I would get to finish my nursing clinicals and become an RN.

I considered my back surgery a success. I no longer had pain, burning, or tingling down my left thigh. No longer did it feel like someone was twisting a knife in my back and buttocks. Despite my studies being on hold, I felt like life was moving in a more positive direction. I was able to decrease the large daily doses of prescription drugs and I only had muscle pain in my back from time to time. Life was looking up.

That is, until a few weeks into February when, without warning, I started to experience nagging systemic symptoms: migraine headaches, stiff sore neck and shoulders, body aches all over, fatigue, and digestive problems. After all I had been through, after all that hard work, maybe I had pushed myself so hard that these were the ailments of an overstressed woman in nursing school. Or was it the continued emotional strain of my parents' never-ending divorce battles? My mother had taken up desperate emotional extremes. There is no need to account the details, but suffice it to say, the police were involved many times. I think it had just felt better to pour myself into work and school so I could stay so busy that I would not have to face all the emotional pain and ugliness. Could my new set of symptoms be the result of stuffing all the stress, fear, and emotions deep inside? I didn't want to start going to doctors again. I was so tired of that. I thought to myself, I'll just grin and bear it, see if it goes away. That was all I could handle. Nothing was going to stop me from my career path. No more doctors. No more setbacks. Just ignore it. It'll go away. After all, that's what I was taught.

Just a few weeks later I got some good news. After successfully completing my third level of nursing clinicals, I could sit for my LPN boards. If I passed I could work as an LPN while waiting to complete my RN course work. Yay! Encouragement and support from the Universe. I studied and took my LPN boards. I passed. My plan and my life were moving forward. I had a nursing license and I had resolved my back pain and sciatica. Yay! Life was showing me some positive favor. I felt inspired and renewed. This was the break I needed. This was the break I had prayed for.

The tone of my prayers and conversations with God were still the same. I would lay my head on my pillow at night at the end of an exhausting day and beg God, that external being outside of myself, to *give me a break*. Just one break. Anything. Something in my favor. I tried to stay positive and upbeat, yet despite my successes, I still felt very much like a victim of life.

From a financial perspective, life seemed to be going in the right direction for the first time in many years. I decided that if I could just roll with this and not *screw it up*, I could be happy and feel good. My other symptoms would go away. Right? That's how it works, right? Don't do anything that will make God mad at me and he'll be good to me. I was being punished for my previous mistakes and if I behaved I'd have good health, right?

I couldn't have been more wrong. After persistent and increasing symptoms day by day, I received a diagnosis in May 1990: fibromyalgia. I remember thinking in my heart, literally in my chest, not my head—I don't know what that is or what it means, but it sounds bad and I definitely don't want it. And in that moment, I refused to accept what the doctors told me. Denial can be a positive thing! I didn't know what the alternative was but I completely denied what they told me. I hadn't gone to the doctors asking for a diagnosis. I just wanted to feel better. I wanted something to do. I didn't want a pill to take. I had already done that. I wanted them to tell me something I could do like surgery or physical therapy.

When the doctor delivered that medical diagnosis, somewhere inside of me I knew that I couldn't accept it. I couldn't become a victim of my body and I couldn't become the victim of another diagnosis. Everything I had learned in nursing school so far told me that the body had these amazing systems that were designed to work together in synchronicity to create a healthy body. I was taught that the body works like a well-oiled machine. What was wrong with mine that it was choosing to create something other than perfect health? What could I do to change it? I had no idea, but I wanted to find out. I refused the medications they offered me. I had been on massive quantities of drugs for nearly two years. I had learned in nursing school about the long-term negative side effects of prescription drugs.

A little voice inside me told me that if continued to take these medications they would ruin my body. Maybe they already had. Maybe daily use of these drugs had caused "rebound" effects. There were so many side effects. Had they been the cause of my new symptoms? Was it possible that my symptoms were all side effects of the prescription drugs? Was this how patients become addicted to prescription drugs? Heroin? Was it from the rebound effects when they tried to quit? Was my body so used to having these drugs that it revolted when it no longer got them?

I was open to this possibility. I was not open to labeling myself with a "life sentence" diagnosis. I was open to rebuilding my body and not putting any more prescription drugs into it. I was open to going through the detox if that's what this was. I thought, maybe this doctor is wrong? I had a reprieve. I had time off from school; my only responsibility was to go to work. I looked for a job as an LPN and started working for a home care agency. I could work fewer hours and make more money. I would focus on getting healthy again and saving money. At the suggestion of several people, I also sought out counseling to deal with all the emotional upheaval of my parents' divorce. I considered that this could also be the source of my symptoms.

When I slowed down long enough to be alone with my own thoughts and feelings, I was sad. I cried a lot. How had life become so intense? So big and in my face? I saw and heard so many things that no child, no matter how old, should have to witness from a parent. It was ugly. Therapy helped me put things in perspective. Counseling gave me someone professional to talk to instead of holding everything inside of me. These were not the sorts of things that one should burden their friends and coworkers with.

I had started smoking cigarettes when I was 16 years old. I began to realize that if I was going to get healthy and "clean up my act," I was going to have to try to quit. I couldn't imagine going through all of these emotional struggles without my *best friend* though. Quitting would help my circulation and lessen my symptoms, but I knew I was going to need help. My therapist referred me to a hypnotherapist and said that many of her patients had met with success with this approach. I was willing to give it a try.

In my very first session, BAM! There it was. The real deal, the real reason I was so miserable all these years. God had worked through me once again in his mysterious and indirect ways, and in that session I so innocently booked to quit smoking, I uncovered my repressed memories of childhood physical and sexual abuse. Now I know some will say that if it's repressed, leave it there; they would rather not remember this sort of thing. But the kicker with pain and illness in the body is that you're remembering it every day. You're just not consciously matching the trauma with the resulting illness. It would take me the next nine years to understand all the implications of how that abuse was now showing up in my body, my actions, and in my life.

I do not suggest that every person living with chronic back pain or fibromyalgia suffered physical or sexual abuse. I'm merely pointing out that for my own healing and recovery, Spirit intended for me to uncover these issues that were buried. Anyone living with pain or illness has their own set of symptoms awaiting a spiritual prescription for healing.

While I can say that it probably would have been nicer if I hadn't had those abusive experiences, I learned to heal them and I consider them a gift. How can that be? How can we come to a place where we consider our worst and most painful experiences gifts? At the very least, I can recognize and empathize with others who have been through similar experiences, and I am witness to the possibility of healing it and moving into what I call the "light of wholeness." I merely present it here because the chances are very high that if you are experiencing chronic pain, you may have repressed physical or emotional trauma stored in the cellular memory of your tissues.

Today, I am whole and complete. I experience life as healthy, happy, and prosperous. I imagine that were it not for this healing journey sent from God, I would not be living the wonderful life that I am living now. I had a choice. At every turn I had a choice, free will. I always had options, though it didn't seem like it at the time. Had I not accepted Spirit at every turn of this journey, I might still be living in a wheelchair! Yes, it actually got worse. I couldn't have imagined it would or could, but it did. And I wouldn't change any of it because in the end I have found peace and joy within myself and the ability to heal myself and guide others to do the same.

I know now that every single one of the "pressure points" that doctors use to diagnose fibromyalgia were filled with repressed emotional trauma. I believe this is a key element for healing any kind of chronic pain. But we don't have to go back through the trauma and relive it to heal. We only have to recognize that trapped emotions can cause pain and illness and are an opportunity for spiritual healing. Taking drugs may temporarily relieve the symptoms, but they do nothing to address the true cause.

It seemed like I should have been more shocked by my hypnotic epiphany, but I think that deep down I knew about it and that was why I hadn't remembered most of my childhood. I spent the summer working private duty home care cases, going to counseling, and trying to manage my physical symptoms. I had more free time and began to date a bit, despite the chronic symptoms of illness and pain. In my mind I thought the best thing I could do to heal was to feel like I had a *normal* life. Dating made me feel normal. It gave me hope. I couldn't go back to focusing on pain like I did before my surgery.

I finally felt worthy; after all, I was a nurse. Nurses are good people. They help others. So I deserved a boyfriend. That's how my logic and rationale worked in those days. I could get from point A to point B with very little continuity. Deep down, I was so tired. I really secretly hoped to get married just so I wouldn't have to work so hard at life and making a living.

Ritchie was a nice guy, supportive, kind, and helpful. He cared for me and was not a drinker and didn't do drugs. There wasn't a huge spark or passion. I'm not sure if I would have known what a loving relationship looked like (my parents' marriage was no meter for gauging that). But I knew he wouldn't hurt me and we enjoyed each other's company. He provided a calm refuge from my mother's emotional turmoil and the pain that was always present somewhere in my body. He provided hope for a normal life. I clung to that like a life preserver.

I went back to school in the fall and finished my nursing studies. Life seemed to be as good as it might ever get, considering where I had been. He was good. Good is good. I didn't need perfection, I just needed good. I would *settle* for good.

I was making an unconscious choice, one that I believe many women will make in their lifetimes. I've seen it hundreds of times in my private practice. Now, don't get upset at me for categorizing and judging woman on this one. Don't shoot the messenger. Statistics and research show that most people who suffer with fibromyalgia are woman, and I think our unconscious decisions play a huge role in this statistic. I believe that we are programmed to make these choices, programmed by fear and societal beliefs.

Later in my nursing career as a visiting nurse, the most common question I got from patients was, "Honey, are your married? Do you have children?" It was, and still is, how many people choose to assess our value or worthiness as a woman. In the twenty-first century, you are suspected of being a lesbian if you are a certain age, single, and childless.

In my mind, as I began to get my life in order and move towards having a stable career, the next logical step was to be married and have children. I just wanted to *fit in.* So I made the unconscious choice that I had been programmed to make by my mother and her mother. Get a man to take care of you. Get married so he can take care of you. There was no talk of love, just that you should marry someone who was "secure and would take care of you."

It would be almost 30 years later that I would find out that my mother had actually found true love in her life, a soul mate, but it was not my father, not the man she married. She had let her mother's fears and dictates talk her out of being with the man she loved. For 35 years she was married and had a family, but her heart was with another man. No wonder she was so unhappy. She had married my father because her mother convinced her that he was a better "provider," that he was more financially stable. But I didn't have this information when I met the man that would be my husband. I didn't see that I was continuing to make choices created out of ancestral fears. My grandmother had instilled this fear in my mother, and now my mother had passed it on to me.

Often, physical pain comes as a result of a lifetime of going against our intuition and inner knowing. In that pain is the opportunity to heal several generations of faulty beliefs and thinking. I believe that when Spirit has tried every gentle attempt to give us a nudge to trust, to trust something we cannot see, it eventually tries harder to get out attention.

The picture and wisdom had been set up for me to see. Don't follow in her footsteps, don't marry for *money,* marry for love. My mom had accepted and lived out her mother's beliefs and fears. Little did I realize that I was about to do the same thing.

I hadn't discovered my unconsciousness. I was still operating from old, programmed beliefs. I was tired and scared of what might become of me and my life. I refused what Western medicine had to offer me, but I hadn't found anything to help me heal. It didn't seem like God was giving me any hope or answers. At the same time I believed that God's answer was my soon-to-be husband.

It seemed the logical thing to do. I had finally finished nursing school, gotten my RN license, and started working in a hospital. With that complete, I could get married and start to build that life and family that everyone was always asking me about. In 1992 I got married and we bought a house. I was beginning to feel safe. It was not difficult for me to convince myself that I felt safe, that I'd be okay. Holding true to my mother's beliefs, I found someone to take care of me.

Deep down, I knew I was not in love with Ritchie. But then again, how would I even know what love was? I just imagined I'd figure it out. At the time I wasn't in tune with my intuition and didn't realize what the twinges in my gut meant. I remember feeling a twinge when I walked down the aisle. It was likely my guardian angels trying to get my attention. But my fears spoke stronger and louder. It was too late to stop the wedding. I didn't want to hurt him.

We make so many choices in life out of fear rather than love. Where in your life have you made choices from a place of fear? Safety? Survival? In Part Two we'll look at the processes I used to get in touch with my inner knowing and intuition and to trust the goodness and love of God Spirit. It wasn't until I learned to do this that my body began to heal and my pain went away.

CHAPTER THREE

I Think I've Had a Nervous Breakdown

The big question is whether you are going to be able to say a hearty yes to your adventure. —Joseph Campbell

Is it possible to hear voices and not be certifiably crazy? This would be my next big burning life question. It wasn't until I started working in the hospital that I began hearing *voices* and *seeing things*. What? Please don't tell me that after all I've been through, I now need to see a psychiatrist!

Once again, it took me several years to discover that my ancestral roots were all tangled up in these occurrences, and to come to see that it was God Spirit's desire to lead me in a certain direction towards my life purpose. I am German. I am stubborn. What we resist persists. Why did it take me so long to learn to not only trust myself, but the voice of God? I spent so much of my life not trusting. I thought it was other people I needed to learn to trust. But really, it was myself I needed to trust. And it was God that I most distrusted. Why are we so afraid to surrender to this loving spirit? Why was I so afraid of what he would ask of me?

I still lived with mild chronic pain and symptoms of fibromyalgia every day, but since getting married it seemed to have improved. I worried less and just accepted it as my new "normal." I had gone back to taking Darvocet a few times a week to deal with the pain from being on my feet all day at work.

Maybe the voices were a side effect of all the drugs I had been taking? Maybe it was the codeine? I knew that to tell anyone, even my husband, that I was hearing voices when I was at work was a one-way ticket to somewhere I didn't want to go. The voices continued, but I did my best to ignore them. It was frightening, not because of what I would hear, but for the sheer fact that it wasn't *normal* to hear voices. And I so wanted *normal*. I had completed an eight-week psychiatric rotation in nursing clinicals. It was definitely not "okay" to tell anyone I heard voices. My imagination ran wild with ideas of how that conversation would turn out and the road it would lead me down for the rest of my life. In the beginning I mostly heard the same three voices. They were kind and benevolent-feeling, but it didn't matter. It's not like they were telling me to do something bad or dangerous. I had no desire to explore their intentions. I was just beginning to feel that I had found a place to "fit in" in this world. No way was I going to jeopardize that. I just plugged away at building my nursing skills and career and trying to find some happiness on the weekends with my husband and my dad.

Hospital nursing was intense. There was a lot to learn and the hospital politics were not my thing; I hated it, but I had to pay my dues. That's how it was back then, you had to have a year or two of medical/surgical nursing experience in order to get considered for a better position. It was stressful. I didn't make a lot of friends. I found that I just wanted to do my job and go home. I didn't want to get involved in all the women's gossip that was a daily event on the unit, and of course that fact alone was enough to set me up as an outcast. What do you mean you don't want to get involved with the gossip and politics? We thrive on it here.

After 11 months at the hospital, I began looking for a new job. Maybe the voices would stop? Maybe it was the stress of all the people in the hospital environment causing these audio-hallucinations? I thought that if I changed the environment, maybe the voices would go away.

I tried to get a job with a Visiting Nurses Association. I thought that would be a good fit for me. I'd be in my car driving around, without so many people and personalities to deal with. I applied for a position with Visiting Nurses Homecare. They abruptly told me that I needed stronger clinical skills and experience. I hit a dead end. I was disappointed, but I couldn't let that stop me.

I went to work at Interim Healthcare staffing agency doing private duty home care cases until I could find a full-time position that I would enjoy. It gave me flexibility. They were mostly LPN-level cases like I had worked previously, but it gave me some peace, solitude, and cash. Money wasn't as big of an issue now; we had my husband's income. But I still wanted to pull my weight and feel of value to our income and marriage.

After a few weeks of working for Interim, I got a call that was unique and serendipitous. They called to ask if I would be interested in doing contract work with Visiting Nurses Homecare! Really? You're calling to offer me contract work with a company that just told me I wasn't qualified? How could that be? Sure enough, a week later I got some very quick in-service training and I was doing home care visits for VNA. I got paid by Interim (at a higher rate than if I had been hired directly by VNA). Suddenly, my clinical skills were up to par. Had God intervened? That was the only suitable explanation. I was beginning to see how things worked.

This was great news. I really wanted the autonomy that this position provided. I would be able to manage my fibromyalgia symptoms better and work fewer hours for more pay. I'd be outdoors more, driving in the fresh air. That really appealed to me, rather than being confined in the stale, recirculated air of the hospital. No mandatory gossip requirements. This was my dream job.

Life was good. I hadn't heard a voice in almost a month. It must have been the hospital setting. And so I went about my life, expecting that this would be the status quo. That is until five months later, when I got out of bed one morning and God Spirit would once again have its heart and hand in moving me closer to my higher purpose in this lifetime. This one morning and its events would change the direction of my life forever, albeit in a miraculous way. At the time, however, I could never have imagined the good that could come out of such profound physical pain.

Standing in the shower that morning and daydreaming about my caseload at work, my life came to a screeching halt. I sneezed and something in my body *snapped*. With no warning, I felt as though my spine had shifted and snapped in two. For the next few seconds (which seemed like five excruciating minutes in slow motion), I couldn't catch my breath, and some kind of energy shot through my body like lightning. I felt numb, dazed, and off balance. I screamed to my husband downstairs. I was frozen in place. I couldn't move. I wasn't afraid to move, I *couldn't* move. He came upstairs to see the problem and pulled back the shower curtain to see me frozen in space and time.

The look in his eyes was horrific when he saw me standing there naked, wet, frozen, and immobilized like a statue. I could tell he was afraid to ask what had happened. We both knew by the look on each other's faces that something was seriously wrong.

"Get me a towel," I murmured. "Cover me up, oh God, cover me up."

That was all I could think, that was all that came out of my mouth. I felt as though my body temperature had dropped 20 degrees. I was shivering and cold. My next thought was, cover me up and put me in the ground. I can't go through this again. Whatever *it* is, whatever *this* is, I can't do it. I looked at my husband and he had this begging look in his eyes. I thought, Not for you, not for me, not for God, not for nothing, I can't do this. I remember hearing in my head over and over again, I can't take it, I can't take it. Wait...that's not me. That's not me answering back. It's one of my *voices*. A female-like voice said, "Don't take it." I'd think to myself, I can't take it, and the voice would reply to my thought, "Don't take it. You don't have to take it." I heard it clearly, but really had no idea what to make of it.

My husband covered my trembling body with a towel and sheepishly asked, "What should I do? Should I call 911? What happened? Why are you just standing there? Why can't you move?" He was so frightened!

I told him that when I sneezed, it felt like I was struck by lightning. That was not the answer he was looking for. He wanted a tangible black and white explanation. In hindsight, though, my answer wasn't so farfetched. I know now that a shift of electrical energy had happened in my body. At the time, however, my understanding of our energy system was limited and I didn't know the significance of what happened. I have since come to recognize this experience and would understand that it is referred to as Kundalini energy. I would not realize its significance until I was looking for a book at Barnes & Noble several months later, and a book on Kundalini energy literally jumped off the shelf and landed in front of my feet. The page I opened to described in nearly exact detail the feeling I experienced that morning in the shower. I hadn't gone looking for an explanation, but there it was. Like everything else God Spirit wanted me to know and learn, it was placed right in front of me, always with the lesson after the fact.

I refused 911 that morning. I would not let them come to rescue a conscious, motionless women standing in the shower. I remember thinking, if he has to call 911, then I want to be dressed. I knew enough about emergency calls to know that there would be a whole squad of firemen, paramedics, police officers, and the like dispatched to my house. I was not going to have them gawking at the crazy lady naked in the shower. If I had to get dressed for 911, we would figure out a way to get me out of the shower. My lack of logical reasoning still serves me well in life.

I directed Ritchie to bring me some Vicodin, Motrin, and water. "And get a heater in here!" I barked, like a triage nurse directing orders. He was so afraid; he would do anything I said. I was the nurse. I knew how to assess and troubleshoot. He trusted that. He had to.

In the time it took for him to gather up my requests, the numbness and tingling that had shot through my entire body seemed to subside and then move and settle in the lower portion of my spine and buttocks. I was able to stand up a little straighter and retrieve my breath. I began to feel the "life" return to most of my body, and with my husband's assistance, began to think about moving my feet and legs, even though I still had excruciating pain radiating down my left leg.

"Get me to the bed," I told him, "Just get me to the bed. Just lay me down." It was the heat of summer and I was shivering like it was 10 degrees below zero.

"Cover me up!" I cried. "Get the down comforter out of the closet."

My husband repeatedly begged me to let him call the paramedics. I don't think he wanted the responsibility of what might come next. Surprisingly, of all the feelings, sensations, and emotions I was feeling, frightened was not "on top." The top layer was confusion. What the hell was going on in my body? It didn't even feel like my body. I wasn't willing to let "medical people" treat me until I could figure out in my mind what might be going on. The voice that had told me "Don't take it" was still talking, and I was trying to figure out what it meant and who it was.

Was I losing it? Why wouldn't I let him call the paramedics? But the voice was so clear: "Don't take it." It seemed so real and life-like. I hadn't figured out if it was real. I was waiting for a sign. I was waiting for further instruction. It was clearly a female voice. Was God a woman after all? Only in hindsight did it make any sense.

Refusing the paramedics that day was the first step I took in listening to the guidance that is always available to us from God, our guardian angels, and spirit guides. This was my first lesson and attempt to surrender myself and to allow divine will, grace, and intuition to move me toward my life purpose.

With a towel wrapped around me, I slowly lifted my left leg out of the tub. I couldn't feel my foot, but I could move my hip and I lifted my leg out of tub and tried to set it on the bath mat. I got one leg out and the rest of my body followed it and collapsed on the bathroom floor. Ritchie caught me and braced my fall. We laid there together on the floor laughing and crying together. I could feel my hip and back, but there was no feeling in my left foot. When I set it on the floor, it was as if it wasn't there. I crawled and slithered my way to the bedroom on my hands and knees like a snake on the ground.

My husband and I were both in shock. Is this my life? I can't walk. What the heck is going on? I sneezed! All this from a sneeze? I pulled myself up on the side of the bed and Ritchie lifted the lower half of my body onto the bed. He got a sweatshirt and sweatpants and dressed me like I was an infant.

"Don't you think we should call someone?" he insisted.

"Yes," I said, "but I haven't figured out who."

He continued his plea for the paramedics. To him the answer was a no-brainer.

I had become a very practical, pragmatic, and logical thinker since becoming a nurse. There wasn't anything that the paramedics could do for me except take me to the nearest emergency room, and I hadn't decided that this was what I wanted to do. How strange that seemed to me. Most people would be on their way to the ER without hesitation, and yet, I was still trying to assess what had happened in my body. What was that bolt of lightning that had shot through me? Clearly my body had not snapped in half or I would be completely paralyzed, but what was this event? What was that feeling? It's etched in my memory forever. As odd as it would seem to most folks and even to me at the time, I wasn't convinced that I would need emergent care.

This whole event from beginning to end, from the lightning bolt to the bed, felt like a full-length feature film in slow motion, but in reality only about twelve minutes had passed. Now that I was lying flat and warm under the covers, it felt as though I was back in control. For now it didn't matter if I couldn't walk. I would just call the doctor and get some steroids and whatever "this" was would go away, or so I thought. I agreed to let my husband call my neurologist's office and my father. The doctor recommended I go to the emergency room and he would call ahead and tell them to admit me for testing. I refused. I knew him from my nursing career and I begged him for some stronger pain pills and a prescription for steroids. He refused.

My father offered comfort and support. He gently tried to reason with me. He had said many times that I reminded him of his mother, that looking at me was like looking at the ghost of her and that I shared her temperament and stubbornness. He knew how headstrong I was. Despite
my appearance, he resisted the temptation to be gripped with fear and panic. He offered pillows and propped me into a comfortable position. I think my husband felt better that he wouldn't be

completely responsible for any decisions I made now that my father was there. Together they'd be able to reason with me.

Once I was lying flat in the comfort of my bed, the pain and numbness seemed to subside. I imagined the drugs I took had started to kick in. As soon as I tried to stand, however, excruciating pain would grip my buttocks and back and my left leg would go numb after only thirty seconds. During the six days that followed, I refused medical treatment. As odd as that sounds even to me, I was okay with it for some reason. I processed everything one day at a time. Each day I heard the soothing female voice say, "Don't take it". I had decided it was the voice of a guardian angel. It was comforting. I had no idea why. I stopped trying to make the voice go away. I liked her, whoever she was.

The only thing I ever heard from her during those six days was—"Don't take it, you don't have to take it"—and she was the only one I heard. I would lay flat in bed. I would get up each morning and tell myself that I was going to go to work and everything would be fine. I was not going to take it. I was not going to accept this pain. I did not want another back surgery. I wholeheartedly believed that I could will it away.

As long as I was lying flat on my back, I was fine and the pain and numbness were minimal, tolerable. I would get up and go to the bathroom, and by the time I got off the toilet, my left thigh and torso were consumed by pain and numbness. I would crawl back to bed and call in to my job to tell them I couldn't make it in that day. I did this for four days, each morning believing that it would get better. I put my faith in what I now called the "spiritual messengers." When I got up in the morning on the fifth day, my hip and thigh were numb all the way down to my knee. I made it to the bathroom. I crawled in pain on my hands and knees back to my bed. The pain and numbness didn't go away.

When I got up on the sixth day, I couldn't feel my leg from my knee down to my foot; it was completely numb. I couldn't walk to the bathroom. I didn't have my usual thirty seconds before the symptoms would start up. I collapsed at the side of the bed when I tried to put my feet under me.

Without knowing all the other significant chain of events that occurred, most anyone would be certain that I had lost my mind. Nevertheless, the voice that I heard was strong yet soothing. There was truth in it. It was the first time in my life that I was really living moment by moment, day by day. As much as there was pain and dis-ease in every moment, something told me that there was truth in the voice and that it came from my heart, or it was at least connected to my heart.

What I came to understand was that there was more than one message coming from the voice. It was delivering information about the past, the present, and the future simultaneously. It was telling me not to take what had happened to me as a child, the abuse. It had told me on the evening of the fifth day not to take what was currently happening to me. It was also clearly letting me know that I didn't have to live like this in the future, or take any of these emotions, painful events, or beliefs with me into my future.

During those five days it was as if I was watching a movie play out in my mind's eye in which I was the actor, director, and producer. I can't explain how or why I knew it, but like a lucid state of dreaming, I was somehow recording all this information as an *imprint* with complete and total recall. And yet, at times I was certain that this was all some sort of narcotic hallucination and psychosis. Only time would tell. I was willing to play it out and see what the truth was. Amidst the confusion and uncertainty, there was a sense of inner peace. I just couldn't be forced into anything.

During the last two days before seeking medical care at the emergency room, the movie script took an interesting turn. I began to see "recollections" of hundreds of the patients I had cared for while working in the hospital. Again, as a movie playing in my mind's eye, every "voice" I had heard back when I was working at the hospital spoke out to me. Clearly, concisely, and in an organized manner, they matched each patient with their medical condition, telling me the mental, emotional, and spiritual causes that had created their illnesses.

It was clear as a bell. All of the information from years ago was fresh, right there in the forefront of my mind and memory, every name and every condition. As I watched and listened, I thought, what the heck?! I had no need to write any of it down. Each voice, each patient, and each illness were clearly playing in front of me. I lay in bed for two days watching and listening to the "movie."

At the end of the movie, the most familiar and persistent voice, my female friend, told me that I was no different and I was also a part of the movie. She revealed that the event in the shower days earlier was the painful memory of the physical and sexual abuse that had been buried inside me as a cellular memory leaving my body. I didn't have to hold on to it any more. I would choose in those days whether to release it completely or continue to let it live in me. With a deep and sincere love, it let me know I could choose. I didn't have to take it.

I didn't understand. I felt annoyed. The message was clear but it left me with what seemed like a hundred more unanswered questions.

The abuse, I did take it. I owned it. It happened to me. It was mine. If it was leaving my body, why didn't it go? Why was I living with severe pain and numbness? Was this why I had what the doctors called "fibromyalgia?" If the memory of the trauma was leaving my body, did that mean the other symptoms called "fibro" were going to be gone when this was all over? What the heck? This is crazy! Was this the only way to heal? Why did God have to reach me through what seemed like ridiculous extremes?

During those six days I was aware that the pain, emotions, and confusion from my back and leg keenly overshadowed my usual systemic symptoms. They paled in comparison to what I was currently feeling.

Finally, six days after my "electrifying event" in the shower, I had to face facts. The messages and movie had stopped, and without that diversion I was keenly aware of my painful situation. I couldn't keep doing this and I reluctantly went to the emergency room. I wasn't able to hobble. I wasn't able to walk. I was barely able to crawl.

After eight hours of laying on a gurney, the doctors came back with a medical diagnosis. Bulging disc at lumbar 5, as best as they could tell, bulging but intact. However, my S1 disc had "shattered." "Sequestration" was the official term. A "free fragment," actually several free fragments of the S1 disc, were floating around the spinal sac. According to the doctors, there was nothing they could do to repair the S1 disc. Once broken away, the pieces detach and float around, hitting the nerves in that area. Depending on where they hit, I would experience the different sensations in different parts of my left lower extremity.

The surgeon explained that there were several pieces broken off, and although they might have been able to go in and repair the bulging area of the L5 herniation, there was nothing they could do to relieve the pressure on the nerves that was causing the pain, numbness, and lack of function in my left leg. The doctor said I would likely be unable to walk normally again. They would be unable to repair the damage. The numbness, tingling, and lack of sensation would be there the rest of my life. I would just have to learn to live with it.

When I begged to differ, they offered slim hopes, along with prescription steroids to reduce the inflammation. He said I could try epidural steroid injections, but they would have to be preapproved by the workers' compensation board before they could schedule them.

With shock and disbelief, I heard a resounding, *Don't take it*, rush out of my heart.

"No," I insisted. "That's it? That's your answer? No physical therapy? No more testing? Nothing? You're not even going to try? You just want me to go home like this?"

The doctor defended his opinion and said, "Well, you did have a previous injury at level L4. This isn't uncommon. Once the spine is weakened, many patients end up having another herniation above or below the original injury. Because this is a 'comp case,' and based on the medical records and x-rays, any further treatment would have to be preapproved by the compensation board. Those things don't happen overnight. It may take a month or longer. For now, this is the best we can do. The longer the nerve is impinged upon, the more permanent damage is done to it and recovery becomes unlikely."

I was shocked. "Wow! Seriously? You've given up without even trying a single intervention?"

The doctor's words and energy felt like a judge's gavel slamming down, determining my fate. His voice began to sound muffled as I went into a fog of denial. I no longer felt any loving spiritual messengers. Nothing about what he said seemed possible or real. I drifted into my own world, paying no attention to anything that was going on in the room. What could I do to put an end to this life? How did I get here? A week ago my life was beginning to come together. I didn't see this coming. There's no way I'll live like this, I thought. I'll kill myself.

Had I lost my mind and sealed my own fate by not going to the ER a week earlier? Would it have made a difference? I had trusted that voice with all my heart. It was my heart. It was not separate from me. It felt like home, like God's loving spirit talking to me. Not a dark voice that was schizophrenic, telling me to do something evil or criminal.

I remembered the "movie" I watched those last two days before coming to the hospital. It was filled with information that could help people. It was benevolent and helpful and kind. It told me that the pain and trauma were leaving my body. What was going on? How was all this connected? Was it connected? Where was my kindness? Where was my "reason" or explanation? Just give it to me. I'll listen. I'll do anything, just give me my life and my leg back.

Why had I felt the lightning? Why did I feel like my body had split in two? That piece kept running through my mind and consciousness. It now seemed to be a metaphor for everything that was occurring in my life. Everything appeared to be a dichotomy, a separation, split into two separate "camps." On one side of life: a dreamy, warm, soothing voice guiding me to resist everything, on the other side—the fear, pain, and hopelessness. Was this my time to choose? What was I going to choose?

The doctor was talking to me but I wasn't really hearing his words. I looked over at my husband to see a tear running down his cheek. I wasn't sure who he was crying for. He had put up with so much and lived with angst and fear from watching me over the last five days. I could tell he felt helpless and deeply saddened. He could hardly speak. The doctor delivered his message and was ready to send me on my way, but I wasn't ready to leave accepting what they had told me.

I was off in my own world when Ritchie took my hand and said, "Let's go home. We'll figure something out." That was code for: Don't make a scene.

When Ritchie took my hand it suddenly brought me back into the room, just in time to witness a strange visual *hallucination*. I looked at the doctor sitting in the corner and writing in my chart. Suddenly out of nowhere a pink and white cloud drifted down from the corner of the ceiling to surround the doctor in a cyclone-like spiral of energy. Suddenly, one of my loving voices now had a "presence." It was tangible, as if I could reach right out and touch it. It surrounded the doctor as if to neutralize and drown out his presence: to surround him with love, and to whisper the loving message one more time: "Don't take it."

I watched as the cloud protected me and separated me from the doctor, as if he was in a bubble that couldn't reach me. The voice and cloud left in a matter of seconds. I was stunned. The voice now had a physical presence! I had really lost my mind. Now I was not only hearing things, but also seeing things. Ritchie looked at me as if my head was on backwards. I think he recognized that I was having a "moment" of some kind, but it was all so overwhelming to him that he too just wanted to get out of there and go home, to find a way to put the pieces of our lives back together.

I looked at the doctor with complete peace and told him, "I don't accept this."

He made arrangements for a wheelchair, medications, and crutches, and sent me on my way. He began to ramble some sort of empathic concern for accepting my new reality and how he understood my denial. Explaining to him that *my* reality was *not* his reality would have been a moot conversation at that point. There was no way I was going to tell anyone, including my husband, about the voices and hallucinations I had experienced over the last six days. I was calm and freaked out.

The next eight months were a blur of pain, ethereal visions, narcotics, doctor visits, appointments with attorneys, depression, marital distress, and financial strain. The workers' compensation board, my private health insurance, specialists, and surgeons all debated, speculated, and argued about the likelihood that I would walk again without assistance.

I lived in a wheelchair or ergonomic back chair with chronic severe sciatica, numbness, and loss of function in my left lower leg, along with the classic symptoms of fibromyalgia. I lived in my living room with a bedside commode. I was unable to sleep in bed with my husband. Lying flat caused excruciating pain. I took so much codeine that there are entire days and weeks of my life that I don't remember. I was mean, cranky, and miserable. And yet, I had many visits and messages from my spiritual messengers that I can remember clearly.

My life was filled with doctors' appointments, and any time I went anywhere near a medical facility, I would receive a message. My messengers would show and tell me what was going on in people's bodies. They would tell me their illnesses and the emotional, mental, and spiritual causes. This was the only time I would receive information. I still hadn't told anyone about the voices or the insights I received. I had been living and dealing with these experiences all alone. Sometimes it was overwhelming. I really didn't know what it meant or what it was for. I wasn't ever afraid of the messengers. They were always loving and gentle. I was afraid, however, of letting anyone know about my secret and mysterious world. Past the age of six, maybe seven, it really wasn't acceptable to have imaginary friends. With everything else going on, I just trusted that one prevalent voice that said, "Don't take it," and I left the rest alone.

For some reason when I saw the pink and white cloud surround the doctor that day, I knew I had some kind of personal connection to this energy or spirit or voice, whatever it was. It had tried to protect and shield me from that doctor's reality, from allowing him to plant it into my brain and reality. Despite the appearances and distress all around me and within my physical body, I had an inkling that somehow I could continue to trust this messenger in my life. I wasn't prepared to reveal it. I didn't hear much from that messenger during the next eight months. I was confused and annoyed.

I was mostly consumed by the pain and medical and legal files of my case, of trying to get the doctors to agree to surgery and to get an insurance company to pay for it. The narcotics and anti-inflammatory drugs I took barely took the edge off my increasing daily pain. I don't know how I didn't become an addict. As a nurse I knew that if I continued with all the medications I was on, I'd have decreased and compromised kidney, liver, and digestive functioning within a few short years.

I would sporadically go to counseling sessions and I think that was my saving grace. Somehow in those sessions I would tap into a small glimmer of who I really was. I just knew that this couldn't be my life. I just felt there had to be more. I got angry at the Western medicine that I knew. They were wrong. They had to be wrong.

Being unable to work for eight months created a great financial strain on my marriage. We argued and I worried every day. Depression set in. My life was going so well before this all happened. What on earth could I have done to deserve all this?

Why had God led me to all that goodness and then dumped me back in this pain-filled loony tunes life?

With anger came more inflammation. At my therapist's suggestion, I attended a group therapy session. About fifteen minutes into it, I knew I was different from everyone in that room. As they went around the circle talking about themselves, I could see that they had absolutely no hope of ever changing their circumstances. They labeled themselves and were resigned to those labels as being their truth and reality. I refused the labels. I refused the diagnoses and the medical terminology. I wouldn't, I couldn't, refer to myself that way, sequestered, ruptured.

It's funny the words that the medical community uses to label an illness. I would come to know, learn, and experience that the medical terms were strongly correlated to underlying, buried emotions within the body. Finally, after eight months of pain and bickering, the workers' compensation board agreed to pay for my second back surgery. I was very excited.

When I spoke with my surgeon to schedule my surgery and pre-op testing, he said to me, "We're not holding out much hope for walking, but we believe we can relieve some of your pain by doing surgery on the L5 disc. We'll do our best and we'll see what we see when we get in there."

I told him that I had something very important and very personal to discuss with him. With conviction and deep sincerity, I asked him to look me in the eyes. "Doctor Kevin, have you ever had a miracle in your medical career, a patient who defied all medical jargon and expectations?"

"No," he replied.

I responded, "Well, that's an unfortunate problem for you, but not for me. Have you ever read about a medical miracle in your peer-reviewed medical journals?"

"Yes, of course" he replied. "I have seen some cases that defy logic and testing that I would have to say are some kind of miracle."

"Well, that's good for you, Doctor Kevin," I said, "because as of today, you'll have a new way of looking at me. If I'm going to allow you to be my surgeon, we're going to have to come to a common ground understanding. It is not acceptable to me that you don't think I will walk after this surgery. I want you to think of me from this day forward as one of those miracles you've only read about, and your first real-life miracle. I am going to be a miracle. It is going to work. When you think of me or say my name, say *Martha is a miracle*. Just humor me. See me healed. See that you are the surgeon who participated in defying the odds."

I was really just giving myself a pep talk, and I wanted someone to share it with me and believe it. Who better to choose than my surgeon?

Despite the fact that I was having visits and conversations with some sort of spiritual messengers trying to lead me out of this physical pain, I still viewed my problems as having a physical cause. I would go back and forth between these two worlds. The logical and reasoning side of my being told me that because the original injury happened when I was lifting a patient, the cause was strictly and only physical and the answer and resolution would be a physical intervention. This side of me would insist the messages and spirit messengers had to be wrong. It would leave me questioning, I must have not heard it right. If it was the pain of abuse leaving my body, why was I in my current condition?

Every day I asked this question. I received no answer.

In 1993 I had my second back surgery. As the surgeon came to speak with me before surgery, he mentioned that, depending on what he found when he got *"in there"*, he might have to take a piece of bone from my hip in order to fuse my spine. I refused. I told him that he did not have free will to do whatever he wanted when he got in there. I told him that I wanted a nurse and a witness immediately, and that I verbally directed and refused to allow him to fuse my spine. Thank God I had been a nurse. Thank God I had seen enough to know better.

I told Doctor Kevin, his nurse, and my husband (my witness) that if I came out of the surgery fused, I would sue him! I reminded him to focus on Martha miracle, and I believed he would be the one to create my miracle with little or no intervention.

SUCCESS! Later that evening, I awoke to find my father and my husband sitting by my bedside, smiling, one on each side of me holding my hands.

"You are one lucky girl!" my father declared with his eyes welling up.

"You are crazy amazing," were the words that rolled off the lips of my husband's smiling face. "The doctors said that things went better and quicker than they planned. They said they will have to wait twenty-four hours for some of the surgical swelling to go down, but based on what they found, you COULD make a full recovery."

I heard what Ritchie said, but I was still groggy so it didn't completely register.

While I was in the recovery room, Doctor Kevin told my family that they were able to repair the lumbar 5 disc. The pre-op films of the S1 disc, taken the day before my surgery, gave every indication that the disc fragments were sequestered and floating around in the sac, pressing on the nerves. However, when they got inside they saw no free fragments, and the S1 disc space, though much smaller and fragile than normal, was intact. They said they had no explanation. They told my family that I was a very lucky girl!

Over the next few days after surgery, every time a doctor or nurse came into my room, they were surrounded by the pink and white spiral cloud! It was back. It had nothing to say. It just followed them and protected all of us. Every time a doctor or nurse came in to do *neuro checks*, I had more and more sensation return to my left foot and leg.

The doctors kept saying, "We're encouraged but don't want to be overly optimistic."

I could tell they were in disbelief, waiting for a downward turn. I thought to myself, are you kidding me? What part of happy miracle don't you want for me? In their clinical textbook world, whatever had been pressing on that nerve for the last eight months had done considerable damage and I may not regain or recover full use of the extremity. Although I had expected the best and was highly encouraged that I had beaten the odds, they were focused on statistics, expecting the worst, and subscribing to the "make no promises so you can't get sued" approach.

When I started seeing the pink and white cloud again, I knew the truth. I didn't hear voices, I just saw medical personnel surrounded with "light." The spiral had a particular new glow to it now. It had light mixed in. In spite of what the doctors were expecting, I had just received a miracle. I felt that I had co-conspired with the loving spirit of God to "send away" the cause of my pain and problems.

During my follow-up visits when Doctor Kevin came into my hospital room I smiled and said, "I told you that you were going to be part of a miracle." He still looked at me as if he thought I was crazy.

I had indeed "not taken it," not taken what they offered as my future reality. I remember lying there thinking, Wow, you guys just witnessed a freakin' miracle and you're still sticking with *your* story?

I was filled with a deep sense of gratitude and peace. That messenger was my guardian angel. That's all it could be, right? Just a guardian angel? I've heard of those. It works for me. I had no real explanation, but the voice had been right. I didn't take it. I had indeed made a choice, *my* choice. Not the choice that the doctors were making. I had been tested. I had chosen Spirit. I had chosen faith. I had chosen a *loving* spirit to be my voice, my messenger, my "God." Is that what this was all about? God was no longer *out there*, separate from me. I had a real, tangible, spiritual, and mystical connection to God?

I chose not to believe the medical diagnosis—all that pain, all that confusion. Had I been given a stay of execution because I followed and listened to that voice? Who was that voice? What was that voice? Was it really "God?" That wasn't what I was taught in religion class.

I'm certainly not telling anyone that God is a swirling pink and white cloud. They would laugh at me and brush it all off as a drug-induced stupor. Three days after surgery I was released from the hospital. Doctor Kevin was dumbfounded, and he did end up calling me Martha Miracle as he watched me walk easily and gracefully down the hall three days after surgery.

When I returned home each day I recovered more use of my left leg, most of the numbness was gone, and I was able to walk further each day without assistance. I was slow and I had some surgical pain, but I could walk!

Nothing would stop me now. I had survived and endured the darkest of days. Emotionally, I felt like I had been released from some kind of time warp. I thought, I don't know what all that just was, but I'm going to get back to my life and take care of myself. God loves me after all. I am grateful. I am ready and willing to walk away from that and never return to that kind of living. I am inspired. I can live with the *other stuff,* the nagging symptoms that *they* call fibromyalgia.

I hadn't seen or heard a voice in weeks. It must have been the drugs. It was some kind of guardian angel and it was over now. Move on, I told myself. Tell no one. I didn't care who or what the miracle was, something had sent that pain and injury away. I got the message. I learned my lesson. I had been over the coals and through the fire.

I really didn't care. I knew I would never forget or take any of it for granted, but I was definitely done with it. I still took pain pills from time to time, but only a little Darvocet. Mostly I took Motrin. I was excited and enthusiastic to get better and to build strength back in my body.

CHAPTER FOUR

Gratitude: The Preferred Drug

When you are grateful, fear disappears and abundance appears.
—Anthony Robbins

My husband was relieved after the success of my surgery. A little bit of light returned to his face and being. He began to have hope. I really felt that he had suffered trying to make things better for me. It was hard on him to watch me suffer. It is hard to watch someone you love suffer. He was truly relieved and grateful not to see the pain and angst on my face any longer. I had a little trouble with some daily activities once I got home, but we were both optimistic for a full recovery and getting back to "living life," free from pain and the codeine fog. Life was getting back on track.

A week after my surgery I got a call from my father's doctor that he was being scheduled for emergency cardiac diagnostic testing. Are you kidding me? Just as things were beginning to settle down, now this? The doctor had sent my father to the very same hospital I had just checked out of. The doctor explained that my father was getting "prepped" for an angiogram to determine the status of his heart. Someone needed to be there to drive him home because he was to be under mild anesthesia and unable to drive. I wasn't supposed to drive yet after my back surgery, and even riding in the car posed some challenging discomfort. Frantically, I called Ritchie at work. My husband dropped me off at the back door of the hospital and I rushed my way up to the cardiac catheterization lab as best I could in my postoperative condition.

A nurse in the lab took me to see my father for barely a minute before they wheeled him off for testing. I knew enough to know that although it was a routinely safe procedure, the angiogram could result in complications and sometimes patients have even "coded' on the table during the procedure.

I requested on the phone that they hold off on the angiogram until I was able to get there to talk with him before they did the procedure. The nurses were very kind, helpful, and accommodating, as was the doctor who was on a tight schedule. I was grateful they had waited and I was able to have a moment with him before the procedure.

In his usual carefree and upbeat way, my father proclaimed, "I'll be fine," trying to ease my emotions. He could tell I was very upset. "It's just a simple procedure. They do them all the time. He's a good doctor," he told me. My father was always light-hearted and optimistic, his most redeeming qualities.

The nurse escorted me to the waiting room. "It shouldn't be too long," she said as she tried to comfort me.

I sat there with a moderate level of surgical pain, worrying about the fact that this was an emergency procedure. That's never a good thing. I watched several patients get called by the nurse, have their procedure, and have their family members called back to be with their loved ones. All in all, it took about thirty to forty-five minutes. I had been waiting for over an hour. No news. What was going on? As my fear rose, so did my pain levels. I walked over to the nurse's desk to inquire.

"Where is my father?" I asked. "Have they done the procedure? What was taking so long?"

As she went back to check on my father's status, his doctor came out through the double doors. He said very little as he escorted me back to see my father. He was alive but groggy, thank God! I could tell, though, that there was something more to the story. My father's arm was bandaged with thick, bloody gauze, like a tourniquet. The doctor held up a piece of white paper with an anatomical drawing of a heart on it, like the kind I studied in nursing school. He lifted the drawing toward me and began to deliver his usual "speech to a family member."

"I'm a nurse," I said, "Cut to the chase. What's wrong?"

"Your father's LAD is 99% blocked," he said. "He needs emergency bypass surgery!"

My dad looked at me, smiled, and shrugged his shoulders as if to say, Oops! Then he asked me, "What do you think? Should I do it?"

He had been my best friend during my recent back problems. He always listened, never judged, and always comforted. I think he was often honored but also dismayed that I resisted so much of the Western medical community. He looked to me as if to say, would you do it? Or could I get a miracle like you did?

I could tell, and I think on some level he could too, that this was partially the anesthesia talking when he looked at the doctor and said, "Well, could I check out for a week and tie up some loose ends, and then I'll come back?"

The doctor looked at him and said, "George, you won't be alive in a week if you check out. You need this surgery now, as soon as we can get the pre-op testing and labs done."

I took my father's hand and said, "You have to do it, Dad."

He smiled and said, "Okay, honey. I trust you."

The next afternoon my father had bypass surgery. I could never have known at the time that God Spirit was directing my path and purpose even through my father's cardiac bypass, that even this could be a synchronistic and divine event. Only in hindsight could I see so clearly how this too set in motion a chain of events leading me to spiritual healing and life purpose.

I would continue to reach towards surrender. I would come to make friends with a benevolent force filled with wisdom. When it comes to pain and illness, if we are willing to surrender to this truth, it will bring nothing but goodness to our lives. It took me quite a while to accept this truth in all areas of my life. I don't hold myself captive to that, for it is our religious and societal programming and constructs that encouraged my rigidity and illusion of anything other than the divinity of my life and of every living creature. In my nursing and medical worlds I was witness to black and white, but I had witnessed the opposite of black and white rigidity when my healing miracle occurred. My lesson was to observe the miraculous nature of life.

I had begun to be okay with the observing during those six days. I didn't rush to make choices or decisions out of fear. While everyone around me was riddled with fear, I was willing to ride out the storm. I hadn't realized how significant this was. I paid some attention to it, but mostly I discounted the importance of it all. I suggest that you not discount or push away any miracles to which you are witness. They are sent on your behalf from a loving and truly magical Universe.

Those storms are your lifeline to your divine life and purpose. We often make it so hard for God Spirit to get our attention and trust. Everyone wants "proof," and yet when God Spirit sends it every day with unexplained miracles, we discount and dismiss it because we feel we can't measure or account for it with science. Science and God aren't separate, but they are measured in two different realities. It's all one, and I for one wish everyone would stop arguing about trying to prove or disprove things and be okay with the "IS." Science believes that it can't measure "God." But I believe what that really means is that it can't measure *religion*. Science has many times over learned to explain *energy*. We see it measured in medicine, in light waves, in the earth's atmosphere. Over and over we see energy being acknowledged, evaluated, and measured. When we come to recognize God as energy, the loving creation *and* the creator that it is, then we see that God Spirit gives us the miracles of science.

God gave us the miracle of Thomas Edison, a living life force in a physical body willing to listen to the "voices" that spirit put in front of him to create the light bulb. God Spirit gave us the miracle of the Wright Brothers to listen to the voices that told them they could make flying machines. God Spirit *never* gives up on us and is always trying to be expressed as itself, as love, greatness, goodness, and brilliance through each of us.

Of this, I am 100 percent certain. I was a little slow with this lesson, but God Spirit never gave up on me. It kept trying to express itself through me, and it is trying to express its divine nature through you. God is not trying to create illness.

A few months after the smoke cleared from my father's emergency surgery, he and I decided to take a yoga class together at the Himalayan Institute. I wanted to gain more strength and flexibility. I was having a hard time getting back to work full-time at my job as a visiting nurse. I had mild to moderate localized back pain and systemic pain and symptoms from fibromyalgia throughout my body on a daily basis. My nursing job involved a lot of bending, sitting, and twisting. I took medication nearly every day in order to get through my work day. The doctors told my father that he needed to unwind the stress in his life. We thought yoga would be a good venue for both of us to explore.

I would spend the next two years trying to figure out how to make a living as a nurse. I was still consumed by the world of the workers' compensation system. Much of my life was filled with mandatory doctors' visits for "independent medical exams" by insurance company doctors. Essentially, their job is to say that the patient is *fine* and to save the insurance companies as much money as possible.

I would try more physical therapy. I had periodic epidural steroid injections and whatever recommendations the doctors and insurance companies would agree on. None of it seemed to help. None of it brought me back to 100 percent and being able to work and get paid for an eight-hour day. Forced back into the Western medical world, I succumbed to just about anything that was recommended to me. It didn't take long for me to feel like I had little control over my body or my life.

Yoga was the one thing that I did for myself that I looked forward to. When I sat in meditation at the end of yoga class, I could admit to myself that I still had a lot of anger stored in me. I could feel it underneath my skin. I could feel anger in all of the pressure points that were used to diagnose my illness. Even though I would go about my day and put a smile on my face, on the inside I was mad at the world.

I was angry at life. I was angry at how things had turned out. I felt like I had reverted back to my victim of life mentality. I was back to taking large quantities of narcotics and lived with pain every day. I was happy and grateful that I could walk and I tried to convince myself that I shouldn't complain or feel bad when I compared my current life to where I had been. I would come home at the end of the day to a husband that was "good to me," but I was exhausted and could only find a comfortable place by lying on the floor on my stomach, propped up with pillows. I never had a good night's sleep. Ritchie tried to help and comfort me in whatever ways he could, but I could tell that he was worn out too. It was safe to say he was *fed up.*

Eventually, after all the back and forth of doctors, insurance companies, and workers' compensation court, New York State classified me as "permanently partially disabled." My attorney advised me that I could now *end all this nonsense* by settling my case. He advised me that payment had little to do with my level of disability. It was based on the wages I made at the time of my injury. He felt my case was worth a lump sum settlement of approximately five thousand dollars.

That was the monetary value that they put on the injury that had changed my life and my ability to earn an income. If I took it, I would never get any money or medical support from workers' comp again. That didn't seem reasonable. Once again, I would choose to fight.

I knew that five thousand dollars would never cover future medical expenses if I was injured again or had a flare-up of my condition. I demanded that my attorney request lifetime medical care related to my case and this injury. It would take quite some time, but I won that battle. That would at least provide a small sense of comfort.

I tried to look at everything through a positive lens. I was able to earn an income, but it didn't seem like I would ever move forward from this. I felt as though this was my life and my reality. I felt stuck! I would recognize baby steps and try to be grateful for each step that I could take. There were moments of positive insight.

I hadn't seen any pink clouds or heard any spiritual messengers in a long time. That felt like a relief. I continued to believe that it was some sort of hallucinatory "angel" from the large amounts of codeine I had taken. I wanted to get better. I wanted to believe that I could change my reality. I had to have hope. I had to believe that it could be different. With all of the doctors' appointments and workers comp stuff out of my life, I felt more in control and had more free time. I focused my energy and time towards my physical body. I desperately wanted to recover the body I had previously known.

The athlete in me told me to focus on improving my flexibility and core strength. My father's heart surgery had led him to the Dean Ornish Program for heart health. He was consistently eating a plant-based diet and taking yoga classes. This felt like a good place to start and we could support each other as we exchanged ideas about yoga and nutrition. It gave me a positive place to put my attention. When I was doing these things I felt empowered and in control of my body and my life. I noticed when I had those inner feelings that my thoughts were positive and I experienced less pain. Pay attention! I clung to those moments with every ounce of my being. I told myself that I had experienced one miracle, and maybe, just maybe, I could have two.

One night before yoga class I purchased a cookbook that was filled with vegetarian recipes from the Kripalu Center for Yoga and Health. It was filled with healthy and appetizing recipes. Little did I know that this was another one of God's simple and subtle divine interventions that would change the course of my life. A cookbook? Really? I could have *never* orchestrated this on my own.

Within a week of buying that cookbook, a program catalog from the Kripalu Center arrived in my mailbox. I had brought the book home and paged through some of the recipes, but I had not had the time to really delve into the whole book and to see that Kripalu was actually a center in Lenox, Massachusetts. A week earlier I had never heard of this place, and now I had received two "spiritual hints" from God Spirit that put Kripalu on my radar. I can't emphasize enough the importance of paying attention when Source repeatedly puts signs on your path.

Wow, this looked like an interesting place, I thought. The cookbook alone had not inspired me to realize that this was an actual center, only a five-hour drive from Buffalo. I had been more focused on the recipes and the healthy eating. It seems that Source knew that it was going to take a few more attempts to get my attention. How on earth did I get on their mailing list? To this day I can't figure it out. Maybe the Himalayan Institute had sold their customer base to the Kripalu Center. But that made no sense to me because they had their own center in Pennsylvania that they promoted. Why didn't I get a catalog from *their* headquarters? God Source had a plan.

I was plugged in and paying attention. I became laser-focused on getting myself to Kripalu. Really, I had no idea why, but I was obsessed with it. A yoga retreat center nestled in the Berkshires? I didn't care what it cost; I was drawn to it. I was pulled. I would somehow find a way to gather the resources and spend a weekend there.

My father's entry into yoga and vegetarian eating had fueled my enthusiasm, and the next thing I knew, I was being pulled by Spirit. I desperately wanted to visit Kripalu. It sounded fabulous. This was the life for me. It was a whole new world and way of living compared to the addicted, drinking, smoking life I was still living. I had deluded myself into believing I was living a healthy lifestyle. Because I was able to walk, I thought I was healthy, yet deep within I knew there was more. My heart yearned for more. I had put my focus on recovery. I had definitely made some promises to God when I was in that wheelchair, and now God was going to collect on those promises. Spirit was leading me to what it wanted from me, how it wanted me to be the full expression of all I could be and what I came here to be. Here was my opportunity, synchronistically placed by

God through my loving connection to my father. It was time to explore this way of living and being in the world. How had I been so oblivious to it?

I had surely experienced some changes and improvements in my physical health, well-being, and mobility. I was not as depressed as when I was sitting in a wheelchair. Clearly, though, I was being led and directed to something new, something I had never even imagined or knew existed! By no means did I consider myself a spiritual person at that time, but I did have this inner feeling that something other than myself was trying to direct my life. Yet I was *still* so reluctant and resistant. I had reached a place where I was deeply grateful to be alive, walking, and feeling better, yet I continued to have a sense that there was more. I was willing to explore what was being presented to me.

Still, I had so much trouble embracing the active concept of allowing and surrendering. I was beginning to have moments when I believed in the benevolence of *Life*. I had moments of realizing that I was in it and a part of it. When I was willing, I could stop pushing so hard against life and just roll with what was in front of me, imagining that it might be something *good*. Mind you, they were fleeting moments, and I often reverted back to old beliefs and thinking, but I had allowed enough of God Spirit to come into me that I recognized the difference between the three levels of existence. On one specific day, I was able to clearly receive and translate this message from Spirit.

I came to understand the three levels of existence to be as follows:

1) Completely disconnected from God Source, emotionally depressed and distraught, allowing ego mind and inner critic to tell me what an unlovable loser I was. Not aware of or open to my divinity, or the true nature of life.

2) Connected to God Source but not having faith or trust that it loved me and wanted only good and love for me. Open but doubting. Asking/begging God. Unable to receive answers from within/God. Seeking answers from outside myself. Other people and healers will fix me/it.

3) Connected, open, loving, trusting, allowing, listening, discerning, receiving. I have all the answers inside me and my healing comes from within and my connection to Holy Spirit. God source is in me and everyone, everything.

After receiving that information and guidance, from that day forward, I was led to more of the truth. I was given everything I needed to overcome my obstacles and illness. I was free to move toward my highest good and purpose. I spent more time living from Level 2 awareness. I spent a few moments back in Level 1 awareness, and I started to have glimpses of living from Level 3. In moments of fear I clung to my old familiar ways, even though they were anything but comfortable.

Two months later I attended my first "R&R" yoga retreat weekend at Kripalu. Two profound and life-changing experiences occurred in that weekend. The first was an energy healing session that I experienced at the healing arts center. I had no idea what I was getting myself into when I signed up for an energy healing session. I didn't even know what energy healing was, but I figured, hey, I'm at this incredible place and I want to learn and experience as much as I possibly can while I'm here. They had only one session available during the time I was there, so I grabbed it. It seemed pretty expensive but I rationalized that there would be nothing like this back home in Buffalo (it turned out I was wrong about that), and I *needed* to do this now.

Later that evening I had my first Integrated Energy Therapy session. The brochure described the healing modality: "Your therapist combines angelic energy with specific hand positions and light acupressure in various locations on the physical body to gently and easily lift suppressed cellular memory from within your physical and energetic body. This treatment is ideal to clear energy blocks that have accumulated from physical, mental, emotional, or spiritual trauma. Through releasing these blocks, you will begin to feel more self-empowered, spiritually connected, and able to move through life more easily."

That sounded like what I needed to get me moving forward and to release the daily fibromyalgia pain I still experienced. I was convinced it was going to release all the pain that was still in my body, that I'd walk out of there a new woman. Of course I was only slightly delusional about my expectations for this healing treatment, but I can say that my energy healing session did leave me with a profound and lasting healing experience.

After my session that night, I awoke the next morning to find that I didn't have any pain! That lasted for four days. No medication, no pain. Holy Cow! This was the first time in years that I went four days in a row without pain and didn't take any drugs. This energy thing, this was a *game changer.* Spirit had my attention. This was big. I didn't know how big, but over time I would find out just how significant it was. What had happened? What was this all about? I went back to the healing arts center to talk to my therapist. She was not due back during the rest of my stay. I was so disappointed but I wouldn't let this stop me. I struck up conversations with anyone I could for the next two days. I asked questions about energy healing to anyone who would talk with me about it. Had they *done it*? What was it about? What was their experience? I took notes and wrote everything down. That was the day I started writing every single day and recording all of my experiences in my healing journey. I went to the gift shop at Kripalu and bought myself a journal. I was being drawn back to my first love, writing. I not only recorded all my experiences that weekend, but I also began to record the experiences that had happened over the previous years. To my surprise, the emotions and details were still clear and fresh, as if no time had passed.

I spent hours lingering in the stacks and stacks of books in the gift shop. I couldn't get over how many books there were on healing and "alternative lifestyles." Back then yoga and meditation were considered an alternative lifestyle, and yet, there were thousands of people who had been coming to Kripalu in droves to study, practice, and immerse themselves in these modalities for health and "higher consciousness." It certainly wasn't anything that anyone in my family had been privy to. It was definitely an alternative to the lifestyle I had been living. This was a whole new concept of thinking, believing, and being that I had never witnessed or experienced. The clear and distinct message I got from the healing session and the bookstore was *Pay Attention!* Over and over I kept hearing the message, *Pay Attention.* It was the same benevolent voice that had told me, *Don't take it.* I recognized the voice. I knew it was going to lead me somewhere good, some place I could trust. It had led me out of that wheelchair. Was this to be the beginning of my second miracle?

During the last two days I spent all my free time from my R&R program in the bookstore. The book that spoke loudest to me was *Anatomy of the Spirit: The Seven Stages of Power and Healing* by Carolyn Myss. It became my new best friend. It was an introduction to something called "the chakras." Okay, I thought, we'll see? It spoke of energy fields and energy centers, beliefs, consciousness, and my ability to heal myself. It spoke to me because on some level I felt that I had done just that when I listened to the voices that told me, *"You don't have to take it."*

I left my weekend at Kripalu feeling almost manic about the new truths I had learned that weekend. I came away with so much more than I ever could have imagined. What I thought was going to be a healthy yoga weekend had turned out to be one of the most profound experiences of my life. Yet amidst my excitement, there was deep peace and comfort that began to stir from within. A deep transformation had begun that weekend. I felt as though God Spirit had been trying to expose me to this *other* side of life when it brought me the pink clouds and voices, but it became clear that I was *stubborn*, and I wasn't willing to take that leap. I exercised my free will by not jumping into those realms of energy and love. Source realized it was going to have to try some other more *earthly* and *tangible* ways to reach me. What better way than to introduce me to a whole community of people who were living the *truth of spirit*?

I had received a glimpse. I needed small doses. As one of my friends explained to me, "You get sidetracked, Martha. You veer off your path."

The thing was now I knew that I could live without pain; I had done it for four days. Something happened in that session that changed how my body responded to pain. I wanted to learn all I could of this new world I had found. Where had this been all my life? This is my calling, I thought. I want to be a holistic practitioner. Everything I was reading and being exposed to had an essence of affirming life, wisdom, and peace. It was the first time I was reading material that eluded to being an active participant in my life's outcome, rather than just a victim bouncing along to the next challenge or disaster.

If one energy healing session could have such a profound effect on me, I imagined what could be true if I followed this energy path daily. And what about the people I could help if I learned how to do this energy healing? I went home to study and get my hands on anything and everything I could. I couldn't find an Integrated Energy Therapist in my area, but I read up on other modalities and I looked for energy healers in my area. I found a few ladies who were practicing Reiki and held some free Reiki circles. I got up the courage to attend. They were very nice people, but I didn't have the same experience that I'd gotten from my session at Kripalu. I was disillusioned. What had happened? Why was it so different? I noticed a very subtle shift and it certainly was relaxing, but now I needed to know more and more. If it was all the same healing energy, why were the experiences so different? I wanted more.

When I returned home from my weekend at Kripalu, I was a completely different person. My eyes had been opened to a way of living that seemed congruent with my spirit and soul. It resonated deep within me. I felt like I had returned home to the

"Motherland." The differences and disputes between my husband and I became magnified. For several years we had been living as strangers to each other. It was not his fault. It wasn't because of anything he had or hadn't done. He was as loving and supportive as he could have been under the circumstances. It was apparent to him that something about my trip had changed me. Within a few days of returning home, my pain slowly started to return. Within a week, I was back to taking pain pills. Ritchie saw a notable difference in my demeanor when I first returned home. He remarked at the joy that had returned to my face for the first time in years, but he watched it dwindle all too quickly.

My husband and I were essentially living as strangers under the same roof. He didn't recognize me when I was a crabby, miserable woman living with chronic pain. He also didn't recognize the new person I was becoming. He was content to remain in the place where he had always been and hoped that I would eventually meet him back in that place. He did not share my enthusiasm in learning about energy healing, but I'd had too many epiphanies and "Aha" moments to stop my new course. I was enthusiastic, nearly manic, about the amazing experiences I had participated in at Kripalu and the new connection I felt to my body and all of life. All I wanted to do was to study and learn, to be immersed in this new life and new world. As far as I was concerned, I had been given a second miracle and I was not going to waste it! I was paying attention. I was going to LIVE! I was going to heal. I was going to create a happy, healthy life.

I didn't know what I was going to do about my marriage. I decided that, for now, the best thing to do was nothing. Maybe he would decide to come with me on this new leg of the journey and open up to this way of living, or maybe he would ask for a divorce. I chose to move in the direction of the body and health I wanted. I'd let the rest take care of itself. I chose to put all my focus and attention on a healthy, pain-free body and a happy life.

With that decision and focus, many of my fears and emotions began to heal. Old family dramas seemed to fall away. I felt stronger and happier. I was optimistic about my future for the first time in a long, long time. But my passive-aggressive approach to my marriage didn't last for very long. The energy between us grew heavier and heavier. It felt like a confining burden. Deep down I knew I was going to have to take action. The day I admitted that to myself, I felt the fear come creeping back in. The questions and uncertainty went racing through my mind. How would I be able to make it on my own? I would to have to move out of the house I lived in. I wouldn't be able to afford it on my own. I didn't want to get into a big divorce battle about property and finances. I just wanted to be free of the heavy energy and keep moving towards my new vision. How on earth would I manage it all? Moving is expensive and physically demanding. How would I physically manage? How would I financially manage?

I was back working in home care and I made pretty good money for part-time work, but if I tried to increase my work load to more than twenty hours a week, I experienced increased pain. I was working on my health and changing my ways, but I still lived with pain every day. When I came home from work I took narcotics and had to lay on the floor with an ice pack or heating pack on my back. Feeling that eventually we would divorce, I was working on paying my portion of debt and trying to save some money.

I had to come up with a plan. On the surface, everything appeared like the status quo. We were civil to each other and tried to pretend that there was still love and understanding between us, but the truth was he couldn't understand me. I didn't even understand myself. We both felt badly about how things had turned out, but we didn't see any way to recover what we had lost. We didn't seem to know how to move towards each other, rather than away. I got paid a premium wage to work weekends because the agency was always short-staffed on Saturdays and Sundays. I had a lot of free time during the week when Ritchie was at work, so I read and studied. I dreamed of a different life than this, but I couldn't figure out how to make it happen fast enough. Setting up a new career would take time and planning. It seemed like it would take at least a year or two. I needed it to be sooner. I wanted it now. I needed to increase my income and improve my health. The more I focused on the journey from where I was to where I wanted to be, my enthusiasm plummeted. It was replaced by old tapes and fears and I began to fret and worry about being able to support and take care of myself. The seed that my mother had planted all those years ago was still being fertilized in my mind. I was soon consumed by the all-too-familiar and consistent stress.

My heart began to ache. I doubted my abilities and worthiness. I wavered between fear and enthusiasm. I prayed for peace. I prayed for clarity. I prayed to not slide backwards into pain and despair. I prayed for my pink cloud. How could I recapture and maintain that enthusiasm and spirit I found at the Kripalu Center? I decided to seek out more support in my community and began searching for like-minded groups.

I made some new friends at one holistic group I attended. One of them told me about a product and company that had changed her life and health. She said it cleared her "brain fog" and gave her more energy. I was willing to listen. She was genuine and enthusiastic about the changes it had created for her. I liked these folks. They were positive and supportive of each other, a far cry from what I experienced with people in the nursing community at work. Most of the nurses I worked with were unhealthy, overweight, exhausted, and burned out. They barely had the time or energy to take care of themselves or their families. This was not the life I wanted any more. I knew what I wanted, and until I met these folks, I didn't know how to get it. I hadn't known any people who were living as I wanted to, until now.

The products and company that my friend told me about came with a potential business opportunity, but I wasn't focused on that. I just wanted to try the product to see how I felt. I didn't want to invest $135 in a starter package, so I asked my friend to buy one bottle of the supplements she had taken. Within five days of taking this supplement, I began to see a notable difference. I was lighter, happier, had more energy. Wow, a tangible difference in five days. What would I feel in a month after finishing the bottle? I was surprised and enthusiastic again. Now I was interested in telling people about my experience. I told everyone I knew. My friend was not "doing the business," but she told her friends that I was interested and within a month I had started to build a new business and income with their help. I rambled relentlessly to my neurologist about the products. He agreed to try them, but mostly it was under duress and to shut me up. Two days into it, he called me elated from his car phone. He found the supplements to be miraculous and wanted to share them with his patients. He had hopes that they would help his patients with Multiple Sclerosis and ALS (Lou Gehrig's Disease).

I was excited and enthusiastic. I felt as though God Spirit was connecting me to all the right people and circumstances. Although it didn't provide a lot of extra income, it was at least something more, and it was fun! I had a whole new circle and family of friends who were teaching and supporting me to live with healthy, energetic beliefs and values. I felt like I was back in the environment I had found at Kripalu. There was no turning back. I was moving towards my dream and I had local teachers and role models to help me create the change I desired. How had these people been in my community all this time and I knew nothing about them? It was new. It was *weird*, but I was willing and open. When the student is ready, the teacher will appear. There had been many signs but I hadn't been paying attention.

What might seem like a chance meeting or insignificant event is usually spirit's gentle way of coercing us towards our purpose and divine self. It was there all along for me but I hadn't believed it. We don't have to get "hit over the head" by Spirit. We don't have to learn our lessons through so much pain and suffering. I know that now. When God and our spiritual messengers have tried the way of grace and we aren't paying attention, eventually they knock louder. God and our guardian angels are there for us always, but we allow so much of the minutiae mind to speak louder and drown out the messages and guidance. I found that even among spiritually oriented cultures we can become so misdirected, even with prayer and the constant asking and begging, while all along the most direct path to God Spirit is through listening.

Ritchie and I had become passing ships in the night. He enjoyed going to happy hour, eating heavy gourmet or fast foods, and gossiping about work dramas. I was immersed in vegetarian

115

cooking, juicing, meditation, and yoga. I was searching for health and enlightenment. He wasn't searching for anything and I drove him nuts. I knew we needed to divorce, but I couldn't support myself living on my own. My health and state of mind were improving each day. I had less pain, but I still wasn't back to 100 percent or able to work full-time. Ritchie started staying at his parents' house and eventually moved out. There wasn't any discussion about how we would handle expenses and finances. He just did what he wanted, when he wanted.

I was annoyed by his actions and infuriated by his lack of communication. We needed to have a plan. I like to have *a plan*. I need a road map (I have come to find that this is a fear tactic of my ego mind in its attempt to hold me back). We had shared all the expenses during our marriage, and I paid for half of everything. I expected him to continue to pay for his share of the household until a judge ruled differently. He saw things differently and chose to stop paying his half of the mortgage and utilities because he wasn't living in the house anymore. There was no discussion. He clung tightly to his beliefs about who brought what into the marriage and how our resources and debts should be distributed. I clung to my fears. I had little or no trust that I would be okay financially unless I could get back to working full-time. While I continued moving toward my new life, I lived in fear every day. How would I survive? How would I make ends meet?

What I have witnessed in my private practice since those days is how many woman of my age and generation have bought into a social fear instilled by our parents. I believe it was created in the days of the great depression when women didn't really work outside the home. I have seen hundreds of women clients who were physically ill and mentally depressed because they stayed in loveless marriages. Dominated and mentally and emotionally abused by their husbands, they feared being able to support themselves on their own. They saw no way out and believed they had to stay in this situation because they would end up homeless. Many of them stayed "because of the children." They did what their mothers did and put up with the abuse, alcohol, and emptiness, like Marissa, portrayed by Jennifer Lopez in the movie *Maid in Manhattan*, whose mother told her, "Wake up, young lady. You have a child to feed. What were you thinking?"

How many well-intentioned parents have yet to realize that guilt and shame don't create healthy, vibrant children who grow up to be well-adjusted adults? This fear and belief of unworthiness were instilled in me by my mother. It would take many, many years to undo.

My separation and divorce process had now begun, but it would end up taking several years to finalize. I lived in limbo. I had a vision and idea of where I wanted to be and how I wanted to live and support myself, but I had no plan and no idea of how to do it.

CHAPTER FIVE

Wham! Bam! Thank you, Spirit

You don't paddle against the current, you paddle with it. And if you get good at it, you throw away the oars. —Kris Kristofferson

In 1995 I would experience one of the most difficult and eye-opening events of my journey and the key to creating the life I wanted. God Spirit would reveal to me the key to reversing the chronic pain and symptoms of fibromyalgia that I still experienced daily. It took me four or five years before I could tell anyone this story. I held so much shame around it. Yet one morning, in a split-second choice, I learned about the power of my connection to a Universal energy, the power that my thoughts have over my physical body, and the ability of our cells to respond to our thoughts instantaneously and consistently.

I was driving to my office that morning when all of a sudden, BAM! The gentleman behind me ran into the back of my car. The impact pushed me into the car in front of me, tapping her rear bumper just enough to shake up the poor little old lady who was driving. My forehead grazed the steering wheel and I was a bit shaken up, but mostly because I was concerned about the damage to my car and missing a day's wages. Little did I know the life-changing events that would follow.

In the seconds after impact I made a decision that to this day still seems so odd to me. What had come over me? It happened so quickly. I still sometimes wonder where it came from. I *decided* to *pretend* I was injured. I decided to pretend that something in my back "gave way." I thought about it. I could sue. I might get some money. I could get out of the workers' compensation system. This would be "no fault." I could sue. I might get some money. That would fix all my problems. It was definitely my voice. It was not the voice of my guides or spirit messengers or God. It came from my head, saying that all I needed was a little time and a little money to create my new life. Everything happened so fast, but I went with it. I got out of the car, grimacing and holding my back. The two other drivers were older, slow, and shook up. We exchanged information. I held my back as if in pain. I said nothing about who was at fault. I called my father and I called the police to create a report to substantiate my claim of being rear-ended. I would take it as far as I could and hope for the best.

I told everyone at the scene that I had felt something "snap" in my back when I got hit. The police wanted to call for an ambulance. The hospital where I'd had my two previous surgeries was only two blocks away. It seemed silly to allow an ambulance to transport me two blocks. We agreed that my father would take me to the emergency room and have me get checked out. Within ten minutes of the accident occurring, I began to notice that I felt different, "funny." I suppose it could have been the bump to my head, but I felt weak, tired. I had to lie down. The officer sat me on the seat of his car until my father arrived, asking me, "Are you sure you don't want us to call an ambulance?"

Ten minutes later my father arrived and I was on my way to the emergency room. I was put into a wheelchair. I was a low priority since I hadn't come by ambulance and was not bleeding to death. I continued to feel dizzy and light-headed, and I had mild increasing pain in the lower half of my body. I felt foggy, like I was drunk. I felt like I was going to pass out.

My father told the nurse and they quickly got me to lay down on a gurney. It would be an hour before I would actually see a doctor. They hooked up an IV and left me to wait. With IV fluids infusing and having had two cups of morning coffee, I felt bloated and had an overwhelming urge to empty my bladder. The nurse brought me a bed pan. Nothing. I felt like I had to urinate but nothing would come out. I told the nurse.

In her own little world, she said, "Oh honey, you're probably just tense from the accident. Try to relax. Rest a bit. It'll be okay."

I grew increasingly frustrated and began to think this was a bad idea after all. My mind was telling me to "just get the hell outta here." The look on my father's face told me he felt helpless. He had been down this road before. He just stood by my bedside holding my hand. He knew I would run this show and that he could only be a loving observer.

I tried the bed pan once again. Nothing. He went searching for a nurse. When she returned I exclaimed, "I can't pee. I've got to go but I can't."

"Okay, Martha," she said, "we'll have to get an order from the doctor to insert a catheter."

Where was this doctor? Was I ever going to see him? The pain and confusion were dim compared to the desire to empty my bladder.

I barked at the nurse, "I can't pee. Why are you pumping me full of IV fluids?"

I knew just enough to be a pain in the ass to those poor nurses. I had not had much respect for Western medicine for quite some time, and I didn't have a problem letting them know my feelings. I didn't feel disempowered or victimized like the other times I was in the hospital with back pain and problems. I felt empowered, despite my current circumstances. Something was not right, I knew that much. I began to imagine that whatever was causing my bladder problem would only support my case for a lawsuit. I did not believe for one second that I had been hurt or injured by the accident. It wasn't a hard crash. We weren't going that fast, only about five miles per hour. We were coming to a stop at a red light. I had chosen to "fake it." What I would come to learn, however, is one of the universal laws of spirituality and the power of manifestation. *The subconscious mind cannot discern what is real and what is imaginary!* My body had begun to manifest what I had chosen to *pretend. The energy and cells of my body began to follow the energy of my thoughts!* My body didn't know that my mind was pretending. I hadn't really bargained for this. I wasn't really willing to go through with all this, but it was too late.

The nurse was on her way to get a catheter to empty my very distended bladder and abdomen. No way, I thought, I was not going down this road again. I was healthy and had made great progress on my own. What was I thinking? Get me outta here. I reached for the bed pan, put it under myself, took a deep breath (yoga move to release and relax muscle tension), and I pressed down on my belly and my abdomen to create pressure on the muscles of my bladder (something I learned in nursing school). After a minute or so, success. I could feel a trickle and I knew it would be good enough to prevent them from inserting a catheter, or at least postpone it. It is a fine line between a patient's right to refuse care and the medical staff being required to follow protocol and take "cover your ass" lifesaving measures. If I developed a complication from urinary retention, the hospital would be liable.

The nurse returned with the doctor and a catheter kit. I refused it and showed her the bed pan. Crisis averted. They sent me for a CT scan, which found *no significant etiology.* They had contacted my neurologist and my surgeons who were both out of town and neither of them took any action or wanted responsibility for my care. My neurologist advised that if my symptoms didn't abate, I should set up an appointment with his office on Monday (it was Thursday), or return to the ER. They gave me a steroid injection to reduce inflammation, one dose of Demerol to control my pain, and sent me home in my father's care.

I slept most of the evening and next morning. That next morning I decided that I would let go of my ridiculous plan and just move forward. One trip to the emergency room was significant enough to remind me of the life I did not want to go back to. I took a few days off of work to recuperate. Somehow God would find a way to bring me my dreams, but not like this. After breakfast and a few cups of coffee to wake me from my Demerol fog, I headed to the bathroom for my shower. I didn't suspect that there was any problem. I was a little wobbly and achy, tired, and lethargic, but I just assumed it was from my ordeal the day before. I had no idea that indeed my bladder wasn't functioning properly. I was still not able to spontaneously empty my bladder. I sat down on the toilet but nothing came out. What? I was pretending, I didn't mean it. Hey, God! Didn't you get the memo? I didn't mean it, I take it back. Cancel, cancel.

I would spend the next three days using the supplies from my visiting nurse's bag to catheterize myself in order to empty my bladder. On two occasions I was incontinent of bowel function. No way was I going back to the emergency room. By the time Sunday morning rolled around, I had begun to show residual symptoms of nerve damage and had foot drop in my left leg. I did not have increased pain, as in the past, only a little tingling and numbness.

I wanted to see my own doctor. I called his office and he was out of town until Monday. When I saw him Monday morning, he was infuriated by the level of care I received in the ER. He apologized and defended his opinion, telling me, "I told them to keep me posted after they did an MRI."

He was shocked to find out that they had never done an MRI. "With two previous spinal surgeries, they should have done and MRI," he said.

Dr. Jim did a neuro exam. "You've got a serious problem! I think you have cauda equine syndrome," he said, his eyes popping out of their sockets. He insisted that I have immediate imaging done and that I take the films to the surgeon's office. He set up immediate appointment. I believed his seriousness. We had become trusted friends. He had been my doctor for ten years. I could tell he was truly concerned for me. At first I thought he was joking, but he got very serious and told me I could go into septic shock if my body wasn't filtering and eliminating toxins and normal metabolic waste. He said it could lead to cardiac arrest. He was deeply and genuinely concerned that I had been this way for several days.

My MRI was done later that afternoon and I took the results to the surgeon's office the following morning. He declared that, based on this MRI, he could not explain my symptoms. He inferred that I was faking it and said he couldn't find anything wrong.

How odd, I thought. I had started out with the intention of faking an injury, but my body had certainly taken a different turn. Was it all in my head? Had I just convinced myself that there was something wrong? If I just forgot about it, would it all go away? *If I had created this with my mind, couldn't I un-create it?* Why did one doctor think I had a serious problem and another one tell me there was nothing wrong with me? Who was right? What would I choose to believe? On one hand, I didn't want to be hurt, but in ambivalence, I wouldn't mind a large sum of money from a lawsuit.

The wheels had been set in motion. How long would it take for me to reverse their direction this time? According to my neurologist, it wasn't as simple as the last time. I couldn't go eight months without bladder function. Why didn't the film show any significant findings? The surgeon was ready to send me on my way. He couldn't find anything that he needed to "cut." Surgeons are very black and white thinkers. They need to see a picture that tells them where to cut. That's what surgeons do: they cut the body to repair a problem. Since he couldn't figure out where he needed to cut based on the MRI, it wasn't a problem for him to fix. He would call my neurologist and let him know.

Before I could make my way down the hall to the front desk, the doctor's nurse came racing toward me and asked me to come back into the room to speak with the doctor. He had been *persuaded* by my neurologist to do some more testing. My neurologist told him that in the ten years as my doctor, he had witnessed some odd findings: my x-ray films didn't always tell the whole story. However, he told Dr. Kevin that he had done a thorough physical exam with "neuro checks," and I definitely had a problem and if he let me walk out of his office, it could be a serious mistake and in his opinion, a life-threatening mistake.

Dr. Kevin now wanted to admit me to the hospital to run some tests. I wondered why they couldn't be done as an outpatient. He agreed and I went immediately to a urologist's office for testing. The test they performed reported to my neurologist and my surgeon that I indeed had *severely compromised* bladder function. With those results, the surgeon scheduled me for an invasive myelogram so he could find a place to cut. It was a week to the day of the car accident. My father told the doctors that I was becoming lethargic and confused, and my memory was impaired. Early Thursday morning, I received a diagnosis: Cauda Equine syndrome. The doctor explained that they could only see the clinical findings when the dye was injected into my spinal fluid and the exam table turned me upside down.

I was willing to let them have their diagnosis, but as usual, I was not willing to "take it," and I certainly had no intention of consenting to another surgery. This was all just supposed to be *pretend.* I insisted to the doctors, "Give me epidural steroids. Put me on bed rest. Wait for the swelling to go down. Give me a back brace. Give me a catheter. Do anything, but I refuse surgery." While I was busy being confrontational with the hospital staff and refusing care, they were secretly admitting me to the hospital and scheduling me for *life-saving* surgery. The next thing I knew, I was being transferred to a neuro unit and monitored for sepsis.

On Friday morning I had my third back surgery.

Wow! My visualization had manifested instantly. I really had a lawsuit. I was shocked. In one ridiculous moment, my body had followed what my mind had decided! That fear-full moment would become my healing and saving grace. Of course, some might argue that I had really been injured in that accident and I hadn't willed my body to do anything, to become sick or injured. What I can tell you is that I have a deep knowing that I could have walked away from that accident in perfect health and without ever needing to have a third back surgery. I used my deep-seated fear of unworthiness and lack to create a way to *manipulate* my circumstances in my financial favor.

There is a lesson buried in this experience, one that is pivotal and must be grasped by anyone living with chronic pain or illness that seeks true healing. Most of the time we are unaware that we are creating our reality from our subconscious fears. It took me quite some time and many tries before I learned this lesson. I have seen hundreds of clients in my private practice who feel trapped by their present job, marriage, or circumstances. They would like to leave "the trap" but the ego mind tells them that they can't, that they should fear financial ruin and abandonment. The energy of these thoughts creates stress in our cells that can then produce pain or illness, and *viola*—we now have a legitimate way out of our situation. Disability or workers' comp becomes our "paycheck," but with a very high price to pay. We are even more stuck when we come to find that these are systems that will never allow us to reach our God-given talents and potentials. It puts limitations on us at every turn.

Years later, as I write this book, I have a clear knowing of the difference between following my heart and intuition, allowing my infinite self to be guided and directed towards my good, or forcing something to happen out of fear. They are distinctly different and so I can tell you with complete clarity and honesty that I'm certain I could have walked away from that accident healthy and whole.

As I lay in the hospital bed after surgery, I pondered many things, especially the decision to create a third surgery for myself. Once again it was as if a movie was playing out. I was watching it from outside myself while at the same time directing and acting in it. I felt as though my past, present, and future were all playing at the same time.

If I had the ability to create illness with my negative and fearful thoughts, and I had used my positive thoughts to not "take" my wheelchair diagnosis, what would it take to use positive thoughts to heal my fibromyalgia? I had sent out thoughts and some sort of divine voice had seemingly spoken and guided me. Why was I not able to instantly reverse my bladder problems? What was the secret to consistency? What was missing? Why wasn't "*Don't take it*" enough to reverse this too? Was God Spirit always speaking and I just couldn't hear because I was pushing the voices away, unwilling to listen?

With those questions came my clear answer. I get it now. The voice of God Spirit and its accompanying pink cloud had taught me, "*Don't take it.*" It became crystal clear. I had been given a spiritual lesson, a Universal lesson, but I had mistakenly thought it was a *one-time offer*. After my second surgery, once I was able to walk again I stopped applying that principle in my life. I hadn't applied it to every area of my life to heal and reverse my poverty/lack thinking and the other pain and symptoms in my body that doctors called fibromyalgia.

I hadn't listened clearly for the whole message. The message wasn't just about not taking the pain and illness. I hadn't listened because I was too afraid of someone thinking I was *crazy*! I was so afraid of the fact that I was hearing voices and seeing things that I never stopped to *feel* its benevolence and kindness. But now I could remember that I felt a strong and deep love and kindness when I was insightfully directed to fight and not accept that wheelchair diagnosis. From an early age I learned to feel unworthy and had been too afraid to be myself, my infinite, amazing, happy-go-lucky, healthy self. I was so afraid of my visions and voices that I pushed them away instead of seeing them as a gift and using and accepting them for more good in my life. I was always so afraid of what others would think of me and I wanted desperately to *fit in*.

Three years earlier, I knew that God Spirit had co-created my miracle that day with my second surgery. My thoughts, which were really just the full expression of God Spirit working through me, had healed that shattered disc. My body had followed my mental and emotional commands, but they had not come from my mind. They came from the *One Mind*, the *One Heart* of God Spirit. I had missed the complete lesson so here I was being taught it again. Another surgery would get my attention. I had used my free will, but not in a positive way. I had used it out of fear, not trusting God to work through me. I had not made room to affirm God's will, heart, and mind within myself. Not in a way that allows the eternal love of Divine Spirit to live in my heart. I had not recognized that "not taking it" also meant to stop feeding myself negative fear-full beliefs about my worthiness and the nature of the Universe. I hadn't come to embody the love and light that God had been showing me, the love that has been placed in each and every one of us that makes us brilliant and worthy, right here, right now, without having to "earn" it.

During the three days that followed my surgery, I lay in my hospital bed and received answers, messages, lessons, and stories from God, Spirit Guides, and Guardian Angels. I was open to hear all that they had to teach me. I surrendered to whatever was going to happen, whatever would come next. I just couldn't take the struggle anymore. Once again, the movie played out in my mind's eye. I was told that when I first started hearing voices, they were spirit guides showing me the mental, emotional, and spiritual causes of patients' discomforts and illnesses so I could "send it away" for those people too, just as I had done for myself. I was told that it was not in our nature to be sick, that "God" only saw us as love, healthy, whole, and complete, as we were created in his image and likeness.

I was told that if I held this truth in my heart, as I did for myself, and stopped resisting with my fear-filled thoughts, I could emotionally create the opposite/antidote to those "causes" and send them to patients the same way. By the very nature of the universe, vibration, and energy, they were sending me the love that could correct and heal the fears and faulty thinking of myself and others. Like attracts like. I had witnessed and participated in this truth now several times in my own life.

It became very clear what they were saying and what they wanted me to do. They wanted me to love myself and to use that love to change the face of illness in our world. They had already revealed to me the spiritual, emotional, and mental causes of people's illnesses. When I first heard the voices I clearly heard the messages, but I really didn't want any part of it. Free will. I think it's funny, this thing called free will. It is always true that we have a choice, yet God Spirit is always trying to stack the odds in our favor and to lead us to our divine purpose. It was clear that they were not going to give up on me. I find this to be true for nearly everyone. This is why it is so important to view challenges, even life-threatening illnesses, as a gift from Spirit to lead you to your purpose. I will admit that sometimes terminal illness is part of a higher plan and there are intangibles of every soul and human life that we can never know, but I believe those who view illness from a spiritual perspective and embody the spiritual lessons from their illness can transcend a "terminal" diagnosis.

The spirit guides told me, "Don't make a 'big deal' of it all, the voices and visions. You don't have to have a *coming out* party." They told me, "We are going to work with you and through you and all you have to do is to hold a sacred and loving space for it all."

I tried to reason with Spirit. They certainly must have the wrong person. I hadn't been able to consistently and completely clear the illness and challenges in myself. I had no right (worthiness) to help others.

They answered very clearly. "You have resisted and avoided us and your gifts. You have resisted your spiritual self and created limitations on your infinite self. Now that you have surrendered, you will clear yourself and be a model for others. You have come to help heal humanity."

I was certain they had made a mistake, and yet for the first time since I could remember, I felt an inner peace, a trust, that everything was going to be okay. I wanted them to stay! I trusted them, and I didn't want the feeling of love and peace that they brought to ever end. They told me that they would teach me how I would heal myself of this daily pain. I was told that my fears and beliefs had programmed me to have these experiences. I had a choice several years ago and I chose not to allow Divine Spirit to work through me. It really is true—God can only do for you what he can do through you. God had been trying to work through me and show me the way out of all my challenging situations. God Spirit had provided many *signs* for me, but I was unable to listen and trust my path and divinity, and in that came the suffering.

Despite the fact that I was lying in a hospital bed, I felt deep gratitude. Despite a third back surgery, I had learned my deepest spiritual truth so far: *What divinity wants for us is so much bigger than we can ever imagine!* I lay in that bed thinking of all the people I could have helped when I was working in the hospital if I had been willing to open my heart and get out of my own way. I had spent my whole life wanting to feel special, loved, needed, and important. God had been doing his best to deliver my request, in his own way, and I had done nothing but resist it. Had I been willing in the early stages, I could have avoided the pain. I have the deep belief and conviction that chronic physical pain occurs in our bodies when we have strayed from our path and purpose and the truth of our Divine Being.

God Spirit is always trying to bring us to our higher purpose, to help us remember that we are created by love, as love, and that by our divine nature we can never be separate or unworthy of love, health, joy, and abundance. It is *we* who create the separation and talk ourselves into our unworthiness and out of our good. Spirit is always acting on our behalf to help us wake up from what I call our "Separation Dream" and align us with our purpose and good. Sometimes it results in extreme situations, but they are never created by God Spirit. They are created by our reluctance to accept our Divinity and to allow God Spirit to flow in us and through us on our behalf.

I was stubborn, fearful, and only half paying attention. This has now become an epidemic in our technology driven culture. There's just so much noise. It is imperative that we learn to shut off the noise if we are to hear the voice of God Spirit. I challenge you to go into any store or restaurant and not be forced to listen to music. It is everywhere. It's nearly impossible to go into a restaurant, retail store, hotel, and the like and be able to shop or eat in silence without televisions or music playing.

When I left the hospital, I felt renewed. It was clear to me that Spirit had led me through all this to be able to help others in a deeper way with a different kind of healing, beyond Western nursing. I was willing to accept my purpose, and from that day on, Spirit continued to fill me with love and enthusiasm for its blessings and unshakeable order and commitment. Having this accident and injury got me out of the workers' compensation system I had been in, and now I was compensated by "no fault" auto insurance. Insurance paid for a lot of things. It also got me into a VESID (Vocational and Educational Services for Individuals with Disabilities) program. They assigned me a rehabilitation counselor who would help me try to create a new career. If my proposal was accepted, they would help pay for training. I knew I wanted to promote health and the healing arts.

It would take me all of 1996 and most of 1997 to work through the red tape of insurance companies. My personal auto policy paid for my immediate needs, medical care, and lost wages. It gave me time to heal, to listen with my heart for the direction that Spirit wanted me to serve. In 1997 all the medical doctors told me that I could not go back to work as a visiting nurse. My private physicians, as well as the doctors who worked for the insurance companies, agreed that I may not be able to work as a nurse due to lifting and bending restrictions.

God wasn't taking any chances on me falling back into my old routines! I tried to go back to my nursing job, but every time I did I experienced moderate to severe pain in my back. I considered it a push from my Spirit to trust our new direction together, and I moved toward becoming a holistic health teacher and practitioner. I also wanted to formally study energy medicine and healing. I knew that the holistic studies and a nutrition program would help me heal my digestion and build my body back. The energy medicine would help me heal the pain in my trigger points and put me in an environment to do the work that my spirit guides had asked me to do. In addition to my own insurance company providing me with medical and rehab services, I sued the man who hit my car and won a settlement. I received a lump sum of $60,000. Now I had some time, some money, and support to figure out what my next steps should be. I still had a husband, a pending divorce, and a house to deal with, but my plan had come to fruition. Granted, I had subjected myself to another surgery, but once again I was witness to the fact that my thoughts had created my reality.

Finally, I thought: I can breathe, I can live, I can make my way into training for a new career. I was grateful to be out of all the insurance hoops and the turmoil of the workers' compensation board. My divorce became final. We sold the house and I moved into an apartment. Peace and tranquility filled my being.

CHAPTER SIX

Truth, New Beginnings, and the Nature of Life

Reality is merely an illusion, albeit a very persistent one. —
Albert Einstein

S oon after I moved into my apartment, I began attending
the Unity Church in Buffalo and began to meet more spiritually
minded people. A friend I met there invited me to go to Lily Dale
Assembly, a Center for the Science, Philosophy, and Religion of
Spiritualism. Their website said, "There are daily lectures on the
wonders of mediumistic phenomena and the basic truths of God
and Man, which Spiritualists adopt as their standard for living.
Each day of the season offers a series of events and experiences
to bring information, enlightenment, hope, and peace to those
who open their hearts to receive."

I really didn't know what to think, but by now I had
learned that when *things like this* showed up in my life, I was to
listen and accept the invitation. I told my father that I was going
to go to Lily Dale for an afternoon with a friend from church.

His reply was, "Oh boy! Lily Dale! I haven't been there in
years."

What!? How did he know about Lily Dale? I was rushing to meet my friend and didn't have time to dig deeper into his knowledge of Lily Dale.

He added, "Stop by my place on your way there. I have something for you." He insisted I had to stop before I went Lily Dale.

I had no idea why, but I honored his request. When I arrived at his condo, he had some old photos of his mother, "Flossie." I never really knew much about her. She died from a brain tumor when I was five years old. My father always told me that looking at me was like seeing the ghost of his mother.

He handed me the photo and said, "See if you can find this house. This is my mother, Florence, standing on the porch of our house in Lily Dale. See if the house is still there."

What!? Are you kidding me? Why had no one ever told me about Florence, (Flossie)? Why had my dad not told me he lived there in the summers of his teen years? Hello?? I had been hearing and talking to spirits for years now. Did he not think it was important for me to know about this? Oops, no one knew that. I had been talking with Spirit. I hadn't told my dad about any of this. No better time than the present.

When I returned home that evening, I stopped back at his place and told him what I had heard and seen that last few years. He denied having ever had any spiritual or mystical experiences during his time at Lily Dale, but he said that he felt his mother had. She loved it there and spent all of her summer days there.

She had persuaded my grandfather to buy her a house there, but they had to be *approved* to live inside the gate, on the grounds. There were strict rules and guidelines to be accepted in the community of Spiritualists.

It was clear that this was again another piece of the spiritual puzzle unfolding, but I had no idea what to make of it. Was I a medium? It was very clear to me that the voices were *spirit guides*; they told me so. But I had never thought that they were *loved ones who had passed on.* I had no concept or understanding for that, and I didn't really care or think that it mattered. All that mattered was that I was holding love for others, listening to the voices, and holding a sacred place for them to heal with God's love.

When I visited that day I expected to hear all sorts of voices. Nothing. I looked for the house that was in the picture my father gave me but I didn't find it. We spent some time walking around the grounds, had lunch, and went to a healing service where they did laying on of hands and a medium gave *messages*. She would get a message from someone who was *in spirit*, a relative or friend of someone who was in the audience. At the end of the service she pointed at me and identified the color of my shirt.

"May I come to you?" she asked. "I have a woman here. I feel as though she is a grandmother figure. She is dressed prim and proper, with her hair in a bun. She is telling me that you have been sick and that this is healing and it will soon be completely healed. She is telling me that you are considering a career change and she says that you should stay on this path that you are on. It will serve you well and not to be worried or afraid of it."

What?! So this is what a medium does? How could she know these things? She was right on. Her description of the woman, my grandmother, was identical to the picture of Flossie I had in my purse. I hadn't shown the pictures to anyone. I was flabbergasted.

On the way home from Lily Dale we stopped at a health food store to grab some snacks. I had never seen or heard of the store prior to our adventure that day. It was in a small town south of Buffalo. As I opened the front door, I found myself in a small foyer that had flyers and business cards taped and pinned all over the walls. A gust of wind blew in, and a flyer blew down off the wall and fell at my feet. It was a brochure for a Healing Touch™ Level 1 course in Buffalo. With all the synchronistic messages I had gotten that day, I had no doubts that this flyer and its content were for me. It was printed on *pink paper*. Spirit continues to deliver messages with the color pink to remind me and get my attention. The moment I picked up the flyer and opened to read it, I felt a wave of warm energy float out of my heart.

I took my first Healing Touch course in October 1997. It was a weekend that changed my understanding of life and our physical bodies forever, and I had absolutely no doubts or resistance within me. After that weekend I knew I would take all levels of the program and become certified as a practitioner of

Healing Touch energy medicine. On day two of the three-day course, I had an experience that felt like electricity was running through my hands and finger tips. It was clear and distinct. I had experienced this one time before, when I was standing frozen stiff, stopped dead in my tracks that fateful day in the shower. Could that have been God Spirit trying to open me up to "the energy thing?" Looking back, that is what my intuition was telling me. The energy healing treatment I received at Kripalu had been my savior and messenger too. Over and over again, I was being led to acknowledge the nature of our bodies, our being, and the entire world, including God....Energy! I was reunited with that energy once again. I was grateful and amazed to be in this place as a student.

My trigger point pain was almost nonexistent after the course that weekend. The results lasted for nearly two weeks. I experienced no back pain. My digestion was improving with vegetarian meals and the blue green algae supplement I was taking. I worked with my friends to turn that into a part-time business. It felt good to be surrounded by people who supported health and helping others in a holistic model.

During the three days after my first Healing Touch course I had increased fatigue and I slept a lot. I hadn't really heard any loud, pink messages from God Spirit in a few months. I kind of figured that they didn't have to try so hard with "the voices" since I was paying attention to all the little synchronicities that were planted in my day.

In early December of that year, two months after my first Healing Touch course, I went to bed one night and had a very clear sense that "someone," a person *from the other side,* was in my room. I felt an essence up in the corner, much like my pink cloud except there was no cloud, just a distinct feeling. I had begun to read some books by Doreen Virtue about Archangels. I had been asking for healing, protection, and assistance on this new path from Archangels Michael and Raphael. So I lay in bed and asked, "Michael, is that you?"

And there it was, clear as a bell, "No, it's Flossie, honey. I love you."

From that day forward, Flossie has been by my side loving me and guiding me. That night she told me, "It's official, honey. If you can communicate with me, you are a medium."

To this day I have never clung to any ideas of titles or labels in an effort to define how God Spirit works through me. I have trusted Flossie with all my heart and being.

Over the months that followed, I felt myself drawn to take some spiritual self-help workshops at the Kripalu Center and I continued to practice my Healing Touch techniques on anyone who would let me. I attended a healer's practice group that met once a month comprised of some fellow Healing Touch students and practitioners, as well as some who practiced Reiki and therapeutic touch. I was attracting more like-minded friends and spiritual people into my life. I encourage you to find a holistic healing, energy medicine, or spiritual group in your community.

What I know to be true more than anything is that those who are willing to be open to the possibilities of new ways of healing have found great success. Those who only incorporate clinical medical approaches do not seem to correct the cause of the illness. In these groups, participants are able to find inspiration from success stories, as well as learn techniques for them to become their own best healers.

Nearly every time I would practice my Healing Touch techniques I would receive information from God or a spirit guide. It was not always Flossie. As I worked with clients, my guides would tell me about spiritual, mental, and emotional aspects of the clients that had created the imbalances and that I could feel in their bodies and energy fields. I would get a clear and distinct feeling or message about whether it was anger, grief, sadness, or fear. Sometimes one of their loved ones who had passed to the other side would bring me a message. Loved ones would deliver information to me that I could use to help them or something that they needed to communicate to them to clear their karmic history. It was almost always about forgiveness. Usually loved ones who had passed on were asking for forgiveness for something they had done to this person while they were alive. It was typically some kind of anger or un-forgiveness that the client was holding toward this person that was creating pain and illness in their bodies. I never said much to the clients. I just listened to what Spirit said and did the energy work. I tried to hold healing thoughts and a sacred space of love, thinking of God and Spirit doing good for them. I thanked God and Spirit for the messages and asked them to fill everyone with forgiveness.

In regard to my own health, I still questioned why I had residual fibromyalgia pain and symptoms. It would take some time for me to understand that I hadn't learned the missing piece yet. I had come so far! I had endured so much physical pain. I was considerably better. What I hadn't realized was that the messages were not just for my clients. They were for me as well. I had yet to learn forgiveness.

CHAPTER SEVEN

The Love Meditation

Nothing is impossible, the word itself says I'm possible. —
Audrey Hepburn

In August 1998 I took a giant leap of faith. I left my job and moved to Kripalu to live there for several months while taking Holistic Health Teacher and Educator Certification Program. For three months I was immersed in a program of daily yoga, meditation, nutrition, and what they called "mindfulness." I was in heaven, surrounded by like-minded people and eating gourmet vegetarian meals. It was a rigorous program of daily classes and study. I learned to be still. I learned to quiet my mind. I learned to listen on a deeper level. I came to understand myself better. I came to face my deep-seated fears. I came to face my anger. I came to face my beliefs about myself and my life. And I came to learn a practice called metta meditation that would change my life and heal my body forever! I wept with joy that day.

I had learned that I could create illness quickly and abruptly with my thoughts and fears. I had experienced some limited success in using the same principles to heal. I had been told I could use that same energy to create health, yet I had not manifested this reality within my own body. I had only experienced limited and inconsistent success. My only understanding was on a mental level. I had not come to *embody* it as my truth and my way of being. After everything I had experienced, I truly believed anything and everything was possible. What would it take? What was I missing? The day I learned metta meditation, I learned the answer.

The answer is Love. On this day the message was revealed to me—all illness is healed with love. Are you kidding me? That's the answer? That's the missing piece?

On that morning in the brisk Berkshire Hills, God Spirit, the "spirit of truth," my friendly pink cloud, returned to give me a message. It told me, once again, that I didn't have to *take it*. But the "it" had changed. I didn't have to treat myself poorly. I didn't have to have unkind thoughts about myself or my body because of the abuse I had endured as a very young child. It was not my pain, it was theirs, and I didn't have to keep it any longer. I could *forgive myself*. It was theirs, not mine. I could forgive myself for holding on to it all these years. Spirit told me to change the story I was telling myself about who I was. I could fill myself with love instead. In the same way that I had meditated and prayed for peace, joy, and love for others in my metta mediation that morning, the spirit of truth told me I needed to do that for myself.

I had tried a lot of things but I never thought about actively giving love to my body. Spirit told me to stop trying to run away from my body and myself and instead to fill my being and body with thoughts and energy of love. With that new insight, my body began to tremble and I collapsed on the floor in my room. I wept with gratitude and remorse. I wept with forgiveness. I wept the next day too, cleansing, purifying, and releasing all those years of painful emotions I had used and held against myself.

On the second day I received a very specific meditation from Flossie. At first I didn't realize what it was or what I was supposed to do with it. I only knew the name of it. She called it the "Love Meditation." It didn't seem too unique or profound to me. On the third day I began practicing it. As I was doing my usual morning meditation, Flossie appeared and began to lead me into the "Love Meditation." She guided me to build a loving energy in my mind and my heart/chest area, and to hold thoughts of love while doing so. I started the meditation with *metta* thoughts for others. I held a specific person in my heart space and affirmed, "May you know joy as I wish to know joy. May you know peace as I wish to know peace. May you know love as I wish to know love." I began to spontaneously think of the love I'd had over the years from my father.

As I focused on my father and the love we shared, I began to feel warmth and joy in the center of my chest. The more I focused on it, the easier it was and the more the feeling seemed to expand and grow. As if my cup runneth over, the feeling began to permeate my being. It filled my chest and then I noticed that the energy started to move to different areas in my body. I followed it. Flossie chimed in and said, "send the love to all areas, send love to your trigger points. Send love to anywhere you feel pain."

I was clearly and gently guided by Spirit, I didn't have to go back through the pain and abuse in order to heal it. Flossie directed me to send love to myself, to send love to my body. I continued to sit in meditation in my room. As I went to each painful area and trigger point in my body, I heard a voice say, "You are love." Over and over again, I heard, "You are love." It sounded like a man's voice. It felt like a man's voice. But I had no idea who it was.

I remember thinking, Hmmm...I am Love? That's good news. I realized that I'd never felt that I *was* love, as a way of being. I always thought love was something I had to try to get or manipulate, not something I could *be*. I never felt I was *love*. I always felt I was the abuse. I was expecting a painful release when I looked inside myself. I was expecting to see all the ugliness, all the unworthiness I felt, all the shame and guilt, all the punishment. But I didn't feel any of that. I expected to see hurt and pain and fear and abuse inside my body and my soul, but that isn't what I saw. I followed the energy. I followed the meditation and Flossie's guidance. In my mind's eye, I'd move my attention from one spot to another, sending it the feeling and emotion of pure love. When my attention moved to a new spot, all I could feel was the fullness of pain. For a few moments it was almost excruciating, but within a minute or two the warmth and love would melt away the pain. As I got to different spots in my back and neck, I wept from the deep sense of love and forgiveness that I felt toward myself. It was cathartic.

I wept as the burden I had carried all those years was released and replaced with deep love and peace. I wept as I embodied and became the truth that I felt. I wept for all the lies I told myself. I fed myself deep love and forgiveness. I wept to forgive myself for not knowing the truth about how much God loved me.

I learned that day that my divinity was greater than any human experience. I learned that my soul and my creator were bigger than any human experience. I came *through* my parents but not from my parents. I came from Spirit. I can live as Spirit and will return to Spirit as I am—Love.

I wept as I forgave myself for the false beliefs I held all those years: The false belief that I could be anything other than *Love*, or that someone or something could take that away from me. That afternoon I embodied my truth. It was no longer only a mental construct in my brain. I became it. And at that moment of surrender, I began to feel immediate release of physical pain in my body. I sat in meditation moving from one trigger point to the next. Sending love to each one, I offered forgiveness to myself and my body. The process went on for two more days, and at first I wondered if it was ever going to end. But I felt that it would, so I continued. I slept a lot as my body recalibrated to its new way of being. Fortunately, I was nearing the end of my time at Kripalu and the demands of my training program were winding down. It allowed me to process all of the changes without jeopardizing my credentialing and certification. When the three days had passed, I was a new person. I was back at home within a week. I never experienced the chronic pain, fatigue, digestive disorders, or symptoms of fibromyalgia ever again.

Over the course of the following months, I continued to allow the flow of this divine truth, love, and forgiveness to flow freely in my body. My heart released the years of separation that I had created with my mind, thoughts, and beliefs. I had no pain in the trigger points. I did the "Love Meditation" daily, sometimes for only ten minutes, sometimes for an hour.

As I moved forward into my new healing and teaching careers, old fears would try to creep in and the ego mind would try to take over. I made it my priority to focus on my breath and the Love meditation. It always worked. I made friends with all the voices and spirit guides and I surrendered and listened to God.

Never again did I pray to God for healing. I thanked God for my body, for the wisdom and order that he had created as my body. I listened to God. I thanked God for my life. I thanked God for my divinity. I thanked God for never giving up on me. I saw clearly that I had never been abandoned as I had always imagined. I was grateful for the peace that Spirit had brought to my being, my body, and my life. I saw how it had always been there and how God Spirit had orchestrated all these events to bring me to the truth of my life and *all* of life: that we are love, made from love, returning to love. I was done with taking prescription muscle relaxers. I was done with popping anti-inflammatory drugs and pain pills. I had successfully moved from being a victim to a survivor. I was deeply grateful.

I was so happy and grateful that I couldn't imagine there was any better place to be in life. I wouldn't have imagined there was a place I could be led to that might be even more joyous. I had come through so much. I was amazed to be where I was. This was nirvana. I had done it. I had healed! I was free from chronic pain. Little did I know that God Spirit wasn't finished filling me with goodness and love, and that there was actually a place I could and would live from that was better than *survivor*. For many years following those days, I was content with being a *survivor*, but God was still working through me to move me toward a more wonderful place. It is the place of my purpose (and your purpose)—thriving! God Spirit has never intended for us to just survive! We are here to *thrive*, as the full expression of him in us and through us.

CHAPTER EIGHT

The Wisdom of Ayurveda

Surrender to what is. Say 'yes' to life and see how life suddenly starts working for you, rather than against you. —Eckhart Tolle

W hile I was living at Kripalu, I had no idea that I would be led to another piece of my purpose and career as a healer. As all information seemed to reveal itself to me back then, I saw it in hindsight. While I was studying and living at Kripalu, I stopped having my menstrual cycle. This seemed odd, but not alarming. I was incorporating so many new health-promoting elements into my daily living, and I wondered, why wasn't my period healthy? Why was my body revealing this imbalance? I didn't really pay too much attention to it. Our schedule there was busy and demanding and the other healing that was taking place seemed so much more significant and important. I imagined that my period would eventually just heal itself on its own.

The Love Meditation was still new to me. I hadn't really thought to apply it to my period. Even though I learned a tremendous amount of information about spiritual and emotional healing, I still resorted to mainstream medicine for small day-to-day imbalances. Holistic and natural healing modalities demand a lot of personal time and responsibility! I admit that sometimes it's just quicker and easier to take Motrin for cramps than it is to slow down, sit mindfully, tune into your body and emotions, or apply essential oils and a microwave heat pack. It is our Western model to just keep going, push through it, ignore it, or annihilate symptoms or discomfort. Even though I had learned so much about nutrition, whole foods, energy healing, and mindful living, I was still often drawn to the quick, easy, and practical side of Western medicine for what I thought were simple imbalances.

Yet, the seeds of wisdom and a larger broader understanding of a true healing system and model of medicine had been planted in me. When I returned from Kripalu I resumed my yoga classes at the Himalayan Institute. While I was hoping and waiting for my period to return to normal upon returning back to the comfort of home, I found an announcement for a women's health workshop at the Himalayan Institute. One of the speakers, Carrie Demers, MD, was a board-certified medical doctor and the medical director at the headquarters of the Himalayan Institute at Honesdale, Pennsylvania. She just also happened to specialize in women's health and Ayurveda. Ayur-what? Once again, divine intervention was at play. I attended what would be a fascinating introduction to new ways of looking at the body and health according to the elements found in nature. I was intrigued and once again I got the message that this was going to be a game changer.

At the time, Dr. Demers was coming to Buffalo once a month to see patients at the Himalayan Institute. On the day of the lecture I scheduled an appointment to see her. Two days later as I sat in her office, I listened as she explained to me about my body type (called a "dosha" in Ayurveda). I was amazed that she could tell me so much about my tendencies and characteristics, since she was a virtual stranger to me. I am a *vata type*, she explained, with strong elements of air/motion, cold, and dry. I felt as if she had known me for years. Everything she said rang true. At the end of our hour together she prescribed a homeopathic remedy and an Ayurvedic herb that I would take for a month. She made some simple lifestyle recommendations for me to follow. Within a week I started my menstrual cycle and my cycle remained normal without any symptoms of PMS.

Wow! Pay attention. Pay attention. As I did with the energy medicine, I began to read and study everything I could find about Ayurveda. A few years later I would return to Kripalu to formally study Ayurveda, and later commute to Florida for advanced training and certification as a clinical Ayurvedic practitioner specializing in Panchakarma, (the Cadillac of luxurious detoxification programs). I opened and built my private holistic healing practice and gave talks and lectures at various businesses, hospitals, and retreats. Over the years that followed I would end up going back to work in nursing part-time to work at hospice and as director of an Alzheimer's unit. I loved the work. Spirit put me in places where I could do energy healing and soothe souls. I often found it challenging to talk about the spiritual truth and energy healing outside of my *tribe*, but I did it anyway. Deep in my heart I knew that for those who were willing, it would make a difference in people's lives just as it had done for me. *These* sorts of things weren't talked about in most health care settings, even though many of the practitioners in my practice group were nurses. It wasn't by any means mainstream. I knew my purpose was to be a teacher.

If I got too busy, overworked, or tired, and let my self-care slide, (which nearly every nurse/caregiver type does), my body would begin to ache, giving me the message that I was about to stray from lovingly taking care myself. I would receive messages from Flossie and my guides that I was ignoring myself and the truth of who I was. As soon as I would acknowledge and pay attention to my own needs, the aches would completely go away.

I immersed myself in the nature of *life* (Ayurveda literally means "science of life"). This ancient system of medicine and healing is said to be the first medicine of the world, dating back some 5,000 years. It is a system that encompasses all aspects of our well-being: physical, mental, emotional, and spiritual. Ayurveda had it all. Nothing was separate. I had arrived at my life purpose: to integrate my intuitive spiritual gifts and my healing experiences with the wisdom of Ayurveda. It was as natural and clear to me as anything had ever been. I arrived at my purpose without really knowing it or planning it. How could that be? God had lined up all these traumas, surgeries, experiences, and healings as the movie I had been watching, directing, producing, and acting in.

It was only in my times of resistance and rebellion that the Western world of stress and pharmaceuticals would look more appealing to me. As I write this today, I have finally learned how to live the best of both worlds and to live from love and joy. I have healed numerous other ailments with the methods and principles I have come to embody (from tooth abscesses to frozen shoulders), and I believe that every human being has that same ability if they are willing to go within to become their own healer, medium, and intuitive.

If I have learned anything on this path, it is to accept myself as deep love no matter where I am on the journey. God Spirit will lead me to exactly what I need in perfect timing. No matter what it looks like on the outside, I am pure love. I do not look to doctors with desperation or false hope for answers, but rather to trust that the answers I need will be revealed to me so long as I am willing to be in the stillness with creation and my creator.

Many times I started and stopped on my path. I looked to other healers and teachers outside myself until I could learn to love and trust myself. There was nothing wrong with that, and it is a very good place to start when we don't have all the tools and information that we need yet. It can be the start of becoming more in tune with your energy and the nature of our world and true being. Even in the holistic world, however, I believe there is a danger of becoming dependent on practitioners. No holistic practitioner should become your crutch or guru. Great leaders don't create followers, they create great leaders. And great healers don't create great followers, they create great healers.

For many years in my holistic healing practice, I allowed clients to believe that I was going to "fix" them. They valued my experience, my credentials, and my successful healing journey. They believed that, by default, because I was so successful at healing my own chronic illness and pain, they too would experience the same results without having to do anything.

That is not how it works, and eventually my God and my guides would not allow my work to continue in that way. Clients would plop down on my table, fall asleep, experience healing, and then go right back out and keep doing the same thing over and over again. It became exhausting for me.

They would come once or twice a month when there was something wrong. My healing energy was powerful enough to provide some relief and success, but it was not empowering to either of us. They were giving their power away to me, becoming dependent on me for their "fix." Just as it is with the model of Western medicine, they believed "Someone else will do something to fix what is wrong with me." Some clients would follow my recommendations for a few weeks and then they would give up. Why? Why didn't they want to do the work?

In my meditations, Spirit answered, "They don't love themselves. They don't believe in themselves. They don't know the truth." My guides continued, "Everything around them has taught them to believe in pain, illness, and suffering. Their ego mind takes over after a few weeks and convinces them that it is impossible and futile to try to change their current situation. If they knew the mind of God, this would not be the case."

As I witnessed with many of my clients, most have come to believe that they *are* the abuse, or trauma, or bad parenting. They come to believe in their unworthiness, as I did, rather than the truth of who they really are. They would go home to their jobs, bosses, husbands, kids, parents, siblings, and get sucked back into affirming their unconscious state of being. They would do the work for a little while and then get pulled into the ego's self-sabotage.

A perfect example is my client, Maria, who came to me one day after we had been working together for six months.

She professed, "I haven't been doing the work. I want to work with you, but I'm taking a break."

She thought she had been achieving good results, but at her previous visit we discussed how she wanted to switch to a different practitioner. She was caught in the trap similar to Western medicine, believing that the healing would come from something or someone outside herself. I told her I would gladly set her free to work with someone else, but the answers she hadn't gotten yet and the results that she was seeking needed to come from within her.

"Do the work, Maria," I told her. She ultimately resisted her own good and healing because she felt unworthy of it. Believing that someone else, a different practitioner, had the answer allowed her to continue to look outside herself for an answer.

I have come to know that just as I was afraid of what I would find when I looked deep within myself, most people living with chronic pain are afraid of what they will find when they look inside. Unconsciously, they are afraid they will find the abuse, trauma, or ugliness they endured and believe that they will have to relive it all over again before it can be healed or released. They don't want to meditate. They're afraid to be still, afraid they will come face to face with all their bumps, bruises, demons, and unworthiness. They believe that the lie they've been feeding themselves is the truth.

But if they knew that the truth they will come face to face with is their beauty, divinity, and magnanimously brilliant soul, they would not hesitate a minute longer. If they knew that they would find the truth and beauty of their spirit, if they knew that they would find love they would not resist. When you come to find the heart of God within yourself, you will be healed forever, but you must be willing to look. You must be willing to surrender. No pill, medication, scalpel, radiation, or chemotherapy can give you that.

Any place that we experience chronic pain in the body the flow of this divine love and truth has been cut off. The ego mind has created a story or false belief about events in our life. They are only beliefs. Self-love and self-acceptance can dissolve the pain that is created in the mind and stored in our bodies.

One of the biggest hurdles I had to overcome on my healing path was the opinion of others who were still immersed in old paradigms and fear-based thinking. It is important to find a group of like-minded people who are making consistent and sincere efforts to change their truth and reality about life and illness. I personally believe that most "chronic pain support groups" are not the answer. They are filled with people who are still too invested in their illness and the dynamics of being a victim. Despite the fact that many participants use holistic treatments like acupuncture and chiropractics, these modalities still leave the patient dependent on something outside themselves for a cure. I am not saying that these modalities don't have value and merit, however, true healing happens when we are able to go within to access our divinity and wisdom for our specific path and purpose. This is not a judgment but rather an observation of my experience within these groups.

As recently as thirty years ago, many holistic healing modalities, along with a spiritual lifestyle approach, were all considered *wacky* by mainstream medicine. With the popularity of the internet, however, everyone has access to books, healers, and education. When I was ready and willing, God led me to exactly what was right for me.

The content of this book shares the struggles, wisdom, and spiritual journey I experienced moving away from the chronic pain and illness and the state of being a victim in life. I moved from victim to survivor. I am happy to tell you that there is an even more amazing, beautiful, and joyful place to live...beyond surviving—it is called thriving.

But for the purposes of this book, I will continue with the tools and steps that unfolded and moved me out of physical pain. It is my sincere and heartfelt belief that anyone who uses them can reverse chronic pain.

PART TWO

The Tools and Processes:

Putting the Pieces Together

Until one is committed, there is always hesitancy, the chance to draw back, always ineffectiveness. The moment one definitely commits oneself, then providences move too.

—W. H. Murray

CHAPTER NINE

Either Way We Choose: Education or Ignorance?

In the beginner's mind there are many possibilities, but in the expert's there are few. —Shunryu Suzuki

Looking back on my healing journey and recognizing the wisdom and insights that would follow me from that time up to the present moment, I realized that a tangible plan had emerged. I recognized that when I applied certain principles, tools, and healing modalities, I quickly became aware of the spiritual lessons in the events that unfolded in my life. I moved through them with ease and grace. I felt the presence of God's grace in my day-to-day living and I became an embodied state of thriving. I trusted life. I trusted Spirit. I trusted myself.

I was able to recognize the three levels of consciousness and see when I was falling back into a level one state of being: acting and believing as if I were separate from my thoughts and actions, as if the world was happening to me rather than me being an active participant in the game of life. I could easily acknowledge when my fearful thoughts were creating fearful actions. When I was consistent with the *practice* of my tools and caring for myself from a place of self-love, I was able to easily discern the best next step or action to take. I could move with life, rather than against it. I could listen to the voice of God Spirit and my guides and trusted that the world was benevolent and on my side. I came to understand that I had been learning and applying universal spiritual laws. I learned to use non-physical, or meta-physical, healing principles that would translate into healing my physical body and improving the quality of my life.

Like the law of gravity, it didn't matter whether or not I understood the spiritual laws; they were precise and tangible. With the law of gravity, if you jump off a 20-story building you will be subject to its principles and effects. You will drop 20 stories down to the ground. It doesn't matter who you are or what you believe or don't believe. The law of gravity is universal in that *everyone* on the planet is subject to it and its consequences. So it is with universal spiritual laws. You may not understand them but you are, nonetheless, subject to their consequences and energy. If you accept that the laws are universal and they apply to you, you can work with them to achieve peace, joy, health, and happiness. If you allow the ego mind to dictate fear-based living and actions, the laws will still apply despite ignorance or unconsciousness. It is from this fear state of awareness that one is most likely to create and manifest pain and illness similar to what I experienced when I lived from that perspective.

When we are conscious and aware, we can acknowledge the three levels of "being." We can assess which one of the three universals fears is motivating our actions, and in those moments we can decide to choose differently. We can apply one of the following tools or healing modalities to bring us back to the truth of who we are. We no longer have to learn our life lessons and purpose through pain, illness, or suffering. We can forgive ourselves for our "unconsciousness." We can "send away" our fearful thoughts and actions and accept that we *are* love, created as "the image and likeness" of God Spirit. We don't have to "be" more, achieve more, or do more to be in God's favor. We don't have to "get it right" or seek repentance from God. We don't have to pray to God for healing. God already sees us as healthy, happy, whole, and complete. God sees us as itself, the full expression of *love*. Our only "job" is to accept this truth and to allow this love to initiate our actions and permeate our life and being. We only have to accept and allow the Spirit of God to work through us as the love that we are. Like attracts like.

The beauty of these spiritual laws is that God Spirit has given every living person the ability to use them and apply them in different ways in order for us to carry out our divine life purpose. God Spirit gives us free will to choose our thoughts, actions, and beliefs to serve its higher good from a place of love. I cannot say that I have the perfect way or answers for everyone, but what I can attest to is my personal application of these universal spiritual laws and how it led to my healing, allowing myself to live a life of peace, health, happiness, joy, and abundance. All I can attest to is what I did, how I applied them, what worked for me, and what I believe will help others.

Universal laws have nothing to do with religion, and then again, they have everything to do with it. If you let old fearful "sin-based" shame and guilt run wild with ego-based thoughts of unworthiness, you will never come to love yourself, acknowledge and find your inner healer, or allow yourself to experience the truth and nature of our world and human existence. If you allow old religious paradigms to invade your belief system, the ego-mind will likely run wild and take over with thoughts of unworthiness and condemnation. If you are willing to accept that God Spirit creates from a field of love and order and that you are in it and of it, then you will find an opening within yourself to walk into the light of truth and healing. The field is not random, as most suspect. This field of love and order is pure and potential energy. Some have chosen to call it "God," but regardless of the word our human minds use to label something so vast, eternal, and imperceptible to the human mind, it does not change anything about its nature or truth. You are created from this, by this, as itself.

I learned to send away anything that tried to present itself as something more real than this truth. I literally sent it away the day that Spirit told me not to take the pain and illness. I was willing to accept and allow the truth that day and I continued to learn tools that helped me change and reprogram my beliefs to allow God to work through me as that truth, rather than moving away from myself and my purpose. I believe that pain and illness are what we experience when we have gotten off our path and purpose and have separated from this truth of who we are, both individually and collectively.

Over the years I tried a lot of things. I read a gazillion books and tried hundreds of recommendations and processes. What I came to realize was that many of these tools, while interesting, did not help me to get to the *root cause* of my pain and illness. I didn't want to manage my pain. I wanted to eliminate it. I wanted to get to the *cause.* This is where I feel that the Western medical management of pain is not able to provide help or answers.

I have included here the spiritual and metaphysical ("meta" meaning beyond the physical) processes and tools that made the most significant and lasting impact for deep long-term healing of my physical body, and which ultimately led to inner peace, happiness, joy, prosperity, and purpose. It is my sincere desire and belief that when applied correctly and consistently, they can help others to remove the blocks that are holding them separate from their own healing and happiness. In my opinion so much of what is offered to people living with chronic pain (even the healthier holistic modalities), keeps the patient "stuck" where they are, only managing the pain. I believe many of the well-meaning holistic practitioners keep clients focused on the *problem* and what is wrong with their body and/or life. Like Western medical doctors, many holistic practitioners have a tendency to disempower their clients by keeping them "coming back for more." It keeps the client focused on someone else "fixing" them, with the solutions laying somewhere outside themselves.

Although I learned a lot of new information in the books I read, I also lost a lot of precious time reading self-help spiritual books that kept me focused on what was "wrong." Beware of the tendency to allow the mind that created the problem (illness) in the first place to keep you focused on being broken and unworthy. My healing may have come much sooner if I had focused more of my energy directly on loving myself, rather than believing I had to earn it. As Albert Einstein said, "We cannot solve our problems with the same thinking we used when we created them." In order to create change and vibrant health, we must learn to take ourselves outside of that mind and its beliefs. We must learn to use our minds in a different way, rather than the auto-programming of the ego. The healing modalities, techniques, and exercises in this section are the tools that I found most effective at reprogramming my mind and body to move away from pain and illness.

All healing is self-healing. Some find that hard to accept. But think about it: if you break your arm, yes, you go to the emergency room to have the doctor put a cast on it, but the doctor does not create new bone or healing. Your body knows how to stimulate its own healing mechanisms to fuse the bones back together. All the doctor did was immobilize the area so that the body could do its self-healing.

By using the tools in this section, you can learn to become your own healer, able to look within to access all the love that you need to live a vibrant life with a healthy body. First and foremost, healing—true healing—is not a one-time thing or destination. Like all of life, it is a continuous process of flow and adjustment. If you try something and you see results, don't stop doing it just because you got better. Like exercise and working out, you can't store it up. So many clients have remarked that they stopped doing a modality because they felt better. That means it's working, your body mind and spirit love it, and you should keep doing it to clear blocks and maintain balance. Such is the case with things like meditation. People feel better when they do it and feel out of balance when they stop. At the risk of sounding a little cheeky, if it feels good, do it!

The order and sequence of these tools are specifically designed to help you achieve steady, tangible improvement. It was that glimmer of hope and relief that allowed me to begin to move out of fear, pain, and illness. Your first priority is to create balance in the energy field, energy centers, and body: to begin to create a steady, even, and consistent flow of chi/life force in the body and mind.

While you begin to restore balance with energy healing, you'll begin the second process: to learn and do the Love Meditation at home to help release the molecules of emotion and pain that have been trapped in the tissues. These tools will help to heal and balance your physical body while you begin to reprogram your beliefs and "old tapes" that created the imbalance and problem in the first place, getting to and dissolving the cause.

The third and fourth processes will help you with the reprogramming of old tapes and beliefs. Simultaneously, you'll use the mala meditation and the Claim Your Freedom process. The mala meditation merges spiritual principles, affirmations, and visualization to assist with reprogramming beliefs that will support your healing. The Claim Your Freedom process combines affirmations with other spiritual and metaphysical principles to create positive change in all areas of life: physical, mental, emotional, and spiritual consciousness.

The fifth process creates physical healing and balance while also addressing some of the major causes and breakdowns of physical health: the digestive tract. It is an area of healing that many feel takes more time to restore (in reality this is not true). I give you these steps to help create a great foundation for making the digestive healing easier and lasting.

Lastly, the sixth process is a simple overview of the benefits of bringing the core concepts and principles of Ayurvedic medicine and healing into your life and routines.

CHAPTER TEN

Energy Medicine: The First Step on the Bridge

If you want to find the secrets of the Universe, think in terms of energy, frequency, and vibration. —Nikola Tesla

I recommend that energy medicine be the first step you take towards healing. It was the first thing that gave me relief from my constant and chronic pain. There are numerous energy healing modalities available to you now. There are many more available than when I was first starting on my journey. Over the years I have been exposed to a lot of programs and have come to form a few general opinions about the nature of what is available to clients who choose to receive energy healing.

First, let me say that Spirit will lead you to the right practitioner for your highest good in the present moment. Be aware that a practitioner of energy healing is only as good as the work and practice they have done. One of the reasons why I am partial to the Healing Touch Program is because I know and can attest to the professionalism, experience, depth, and certification process of its teachers and practitioners. You will attract the level of practitioner that you are willing to accept and work with. If you believe that you need to start out slow, you will attract that. If you believe you are ready to embrace complete and quick healing and change, you can attract that as well. Be aware and be very clear of your intention when you seek a practitioner. If you just want to *dabble a bit*, you will find someone who will help you dabble. If you want to get to the core of what is holding you stuck in pain, illness, or a lackluster life, then set your intention for that. The choice is always up to you!

The most well-known or "heard of" therapy is Reiki. A word of caution however: most "well-known" doesn't necessarily mean that it is the best choice. Just because someone is a Reiki master or teacher does not mean they have done their work. I know many Reiki practitioners who take the course and get attuned but never actually do the healing work on themselves or others. They have not become proficient in learning the dynamic principles of energy medicine as a whole. It can be like taking courses in medical school but never completing residency, being in the trenches and getting the real experience of practicing medicine.

The Healing Touch Program is the only program (at the time of this writing) that is accredited as an energy medicine therapy and program. The Healing Touch Program was first taught as a continuing education course for nurses, and it still maintains a rigorous and well-grounded curriculum to become a certified practitioner. I do not intend to say that other modalities aren't effective or without a good training program. In my 26 years in this industry I have witnessed and mentored many practitioners from other programs who were not trained to "manage energy" and are not skilled in providing a therapeutic experience for clients.

Do your research! Ask questions of the practitioners with whom you are considering working. If money is an issue, don't just go to someone because their rates are cheaper. In this case you will definitely get what you pay for. Look for a practitioner who has advanced studies and certifications in their modalities. Ask them where they have worked and for how long. When certain modalities become popular and well known, there are always hundreds of folks who want to jump on the bandwagon just to add another set of letters to the end of their name; that doesn't mean that they have achieved proficiency or skills. Look for practitioners who are established and well known in your community. Many healing practitioners work as independent contractors at spas and health centers. Inquire about their skills and professionalism from previous facilities where they worked. Ask for testimonials and referrals from people who have worked with them. Are they helping their clients get the same kinds of results that you are looking for? Do they have a specialty area? Do they specialize in chronic pain or illness? I took advanced courses in energy medicine and I learned to palpate the energy and vibration of the valves of the digestive tract. As strange as that sounds, it allows me to help clients with reflux and GERD to get tangible relief from their symptoms, and it is something that I was well-known for in my practice and community.

Once you choose a practitioner, stick with them for at least six months. Be honest with them, and be honest with yourself. Be willing to be open to new ideas and suggestions. If what you know and what you have been doing had worked, you wouldn't be in the state that you are in now. Remember, the definition of insanity is doing the same thing over and over and expecting to get different results. Why do I recommend energy healing (and specifically, Healing Touch)?

Healing Touch is a collection of over thirty different techniques of energy healing that offer specific treatments for specific problems. Some are focused treatments (specific to things like migraines or sinus headaches), and others are general *balancing* treatments or what are called "full-body." For example, you may go to a practitioner because you're suffering from migraine headaches. She has specific techniques for migraine relief, as well as a full-body technique to balance the whole body, reduce stress (a major contributor to migraines), and open blocked or congested areas throughout the whole body and energy field. For more information about the Healing Touch Program or practitioners, see the resources section.

A very important factor in my complete reversal of chronic pain was my ability to perceive and feel energy moving in my body. Because of this, I also recommend that you don't just receive energy healing treatments, but that you also learn to feel and sense energy for yourself within your own body. I strongly suggest you take at least one Healing Touch course. This is a crucial and critical component of becoming your own best healer. It empowers YOU. It shifts the responsibility for the outcome to you rather than being at the mercy of a doctor or another practitioner to tell you how it is or how *they* think it's going to be.

I believe that our entire world is currently in a paradigm shift as more and more people are waking up to their ability to sense and feel different levels of energy within themselves and others. Everyone has the ability to feel energy! We are all made of energy, from the same energy, and we are living in a field of energy, so it *is* our nature. To FEEL our own energy is to feel our own nature, our life force, our intuition, and our divinity. It is to feel the spirit that feeds our own hearts. The gift that I came to learn and understand in feeling energy is that we don't need to read a bunch of books or take a million courses that keep us up in our heads. We need to learn to trust our FEELINGS and connect to our "source," which is a field of loving energy. This is the source of true and complete healing.

This may seem like a foreign concept for many, but it is not new. Think about it. Our hearts beat with absolutely no effort on our part. Our lungs rise and fall as the breath moves in and out of our bodies, with no effort from us. When a medical doctor wants to measure the efficiency of our hearts, they perform an *electro*-cardiogram. When they want to measure the functioning of our brains, they perform an *electro*-encephalogram. What are they measuring in these tests? They're measuring the amount and direction of the waves of energy that the organs are emitting. In the heart the doctors measure the S wave or the Q wave. If they find an abnormality, they prescribe a beta-blocker or a calcium channel-blocker, drugs that change the *frequency* of the electricity flowing in the heart to cause it to behave differently. Yet, the interesting thing to note is that when they perform these tests, the electrodes are on the *outside* of the body. So we can easily draw the conclusion that the outside of our body is a conductor for the energy on the inside of our body. This is the basic premise for the success and principles of energy healing. With practice, you can and will learn how to feel and manage this energy for yourself to become your own healer.

We are incredible bundles of energy. Although much of Western medicine tries to invalidate what they consider to be "new age" or *placebo* healing, they ignore their own beliefs and science: that we are bundles of energy. Our physical bodies are essentially finely tuned systems that respond to all principles of energy.

Have you ever thought about how or why we have static electricity in our hair, or how we can transfer an electrical shock to another person or a door knob? We've all had that happen. In order for it to happen, we must be conductors and receivers of electrical energy.

It is important for you to begin to learn and understand the concepts of energy medicine and energy healing. Don't wait a minute longer and don't dismiss the idea, saying to yourself, "If this stuff worked, why don't the doctors tell you about it?" There are many factors that go into what doctors subscribe to and much of it has to do with profits and pharmaceutical companies. Remember that, to date, what mainstream medicine has offered you and millions of patients has not helped to stop the epidemic of chronic pain and illness. They have only offered to manage it. Isn't it worth a look to stop living in the world of symptom management and move towards vibrant health?

ENERGY PRINCIPLES
- Energy permeates all animate and inanimate matter.
- All healing is self-healing. However, it can be assisted by others.
- Human beings are composed of interpenetrating layers or fields of energy and each layer vibrates to a different frequency.
- The world and everything in it are interdependent.
- A person can influence the energy system without being able to feel or see it.
- All life experiences are recorded and stored within the energy system.
- Potential illness appears in the energy system before signs of illness appear.
- A person's health and quality of life are affected by the health and quality of their energy system, and vice versa.

- Our energy systems are influenced by the environment, thoughts, emotions, actions, and intentionality.
- Energy can be experienced as movement, temperature, or density.

Many energy healing modalities work with the energy centers (called "chakras") and the layers of the bio-energy field (referred to as "aura"). While it is important to have a basic understanding of these concepts, I don't recommend getting immersed or lost in an in-depth assessment of your chakras or energy field, as many tend to get stuck or lost there, as I did, putting their attention on the problem instead of the solution.

It is enough to have some knowledge and awareness of where you might have an imbalance, but don't focus on that! Do the Love meditation, which follows, with any area of imbalance that you or any practitioner uncover, while also doing some energy healing. Do not spend time focusing on your imbalances, but affirm that you are creating balance throughout your entire body. More about how to do that follows.

CHAPTER ELEVEN

Becoming the Love Meditation

You are never alone and helpless. The force that guides the stars guides you too. —Shrii Shrii Anandamurti

The Love meditation is a healing meditation that was channeled to me from one of my spirit guides. It was effective in helping me eliminate all of the pain in my pressure points and the rest of my body. I continue to use it today, as do many of my clients. It is so simple that often clients have dismissed its efficiency and validity. They can't imagine that something so simple could be the solution to their pain or illness. Some are still living in a state of unawareness, not realizing that they hold the key to their healing, not the doctors.

Before I tell you how to do the love meditation, I want to explain some of the core concepts behind its effectiveness. As I've mentioned, when working in the spiritual realm, "what we resist persists." Pain and illness manifest as an opportunity for spiritual growth to bring us back to the truth of who we are, and to move us back in the direction of our life purpose. Chronic pain and illness manifest in an attempt to get our attention and to teach lessons that will lead us back to your higher self. If we remain unaware and continue to resist this spiritual truth, we are resisting and moving away from love and our true self. The success of healing with the Love Meditation is due to the fact that it dissolves our resistance with love, not fear. Rather than move away from or masking the pain or illness, the Love meditation moves you toward it so that it can be resolved and released from the physical body. When you sit in stillness and move toward the illness or discomfort, God Spirit has an opportunity to be heard (over the voice of the ego) to deliver messages that have the ability to move you back toward your health, divinity and purpose. The Love Meditation teaches you to listen to God Spirit for direction and guidance, rather than begging and praying to God for healing out of desperation. It teaches you to acknowledge and allow God to move through you and within you, rather than as something outside and separate from you. It brings you to a place of surrender and trust in God and your divine nature.

Medical approaches of surgery and drugs try to drown out the pain, making it impossible to access or receive the spiritual message. The reason that prescription pain medications haven't been successful at relieving chronic pain is they are not spiritually attuned. God Spirit never forsakes us in trying to deliver its message for our highest good. Medications and surgery are unable to drown out God Spirit's attempt to reach us. If they could, we wouldn't still be living with pain. Pain and illness remain as Spirit's way to tell us that we are out of touch and out of balance with our divine selves, usually clinging to one of the three universal fears.

The meditation: Sit in a quiet and comfortable place. It can be in a chair or a meditation cushion. If you are an experienced meditator, you may choose to sit on the floor, cross-legged on a cushion. If you are new to meditation, you may choose to sit in a chair with both feet planted flat and firmly on the floor. You may choose to light a candle and play some soft music to relax you.

1. Begin to bring your awareness to your breath. With each breath in, feel the cool air that comes in through your nostrils. Don't try to change or create anything, just observe the body and the breath and how they move together. Allow yourself to sit in this awareness for a few minutes.

2. After a few minutes, bring your awareness to your chest and your heart center. Notice the subtle rise and fall of the chest with each breath. Observe with each inhalation the lungs inflating and expanding. Observe with the exhalation the chest and abdomen lowering and contracting to force the air out of the body. Allow yourself to sit in this present moment to become more aware of the rhythm and flow of your body, bringing your attention out of your head and into your physical body

3. As you begin to relax while you observe your breath, bring your awareness to your feet making contact with the floor. Take a few breaths while focusing on the bottoms of your

feet. Now draw your awareness to your hips and buttocks. Feel the points of contact that they make with the chair or the floor. Allow the breath to relax and soften those areas. Bring your awareness to your spine, relaxing the tension from each vertebra on by one. Arriving at your shoulders, continue to focus on the calming rhythm of your breath as you allow your shoulders to drop. Notice the palms of your hands and where they make contact with your lap or your chair. Feel the warmth in the palms of your hands as you bring your awareness to them. Allow your breath to relax your hands and your arms, continuing to observe the rise and fall of your chest as you gently breathe in and out. Allow the warmth in your hands to flow up your arms to your shoulders and eventually arrive back at your chest and your heart center.

4. Bring your attention and your focus to your heart and breathe into the center of your chest. As you breathe in, draw your awareness to your chest and imagine that the sun is in your chest as a warm, golden ball of light. Feel it soothing, relaxing, and warming your heart and your chest. With each breath in, feel its healing warm light filling you up with peace and joy, radiating out into your whole body. As the warm, golden, white sunlight fills you up, remember a person, place, or situation that has brought you a feeling and sense of deep love. This can be a pet, spouse, cherished friend, or even someone who has passed on, or it could be the memory of a

wonderful vacation or your children, whatever brings you and your heart the FEELING of love, peace, and joy. Allow yourself to be immersed in that feeling of love and joy as you continue to bring your breath to your heart center. Allow the feeling to expand and radiate the ball of sunshine with the rhythm of your breath. Feel the feeling of love in your chest. Feel the warmth, feel the joy, feel the peace. This is who you are. You are love. Repeat and affirm to yourself while staying present to this feeling in your chest, *I am love*. Allow the feeling to expand and repeat to yourself, *I am love*. Expand the affirmation and say, *I am the full expression of God's love. God is love. I am love*. Stay with the feeling by remembering the person or situation that brings you that deep sense of love (Hint: your ego mind will try to talk you out of this place and feeling).

5. Do this meditation every morning and every evening until it becomes easier and easier to relax yourself and your mind and to drop into this state of feeling love, peace, and joy in the center of your chest and to affirm *I am love*. There is no hurry or time limit. Just continue to do the meditation. It is working even though you may not think so. When you consistently allow this feeling of love and affirm that you are love, that you are the full expression of God's love, you are ready to start using that feeling to dissolve the areas of illness or pain.

6. After you have practiced the love meditation and are comfortable with doing it, begin the meditation by asking God Spirit to reveal any information you need to help your healing to occur. Affirm to Spirit that you are ready to send away any false beliefs that have been stored. Affirm that you are love and you are ready to hear Spirit's message of love for you and your highest good. If you find yourself getting anxious or distracted, just keep bringing your attention back to the center of your chest and focus on the person, thing, or event that makes you feel deep love while continuing to observe your breath. When you are in this state, take that feeling of love and warmth and draw it or move it with your breath and attention to any area of pain or illness. For example, if you have a painful frozen shoulder, move it there. Focus the feeling of love and sunshine and warmth there. Affirm *I am love, God is love, I am the full expression of God's love* while focusing the feeling of love and warmth on your shoulder. If you have diabetes, do the same thing while bringing your attention to the area of the pancreas in the right upper and back abdomen.

The more you do this exercise, the more you will begin to feel a change and shift in the area. At first you may feel more pain or extreme heat because you are bringing awareness to it instead of trying to drown it out. This is temporary. It will pass.

Continue to do the meditation and ask God Spirit, as if in prayer, do you have any loving messages for me from this part of my body? You may get an insight. You may feel fear well up. You may feel anger, shame, or guilt start to well up where you were previously feeling the love. Make a note of the sensation or emotion, (it's a good idea to have a journal close by), and then go back to filling the area with love, sunshine, and warmth while affirming *I am love, God is love, I am the full expression of God's love*. You may see a color in your mind's eye, or several colors. Just make a note of it and then continue the meditation. You can talk to the area while still allowing the feeling of love to expand there. Ask it what it wants to tell you while affirming that you are love. It is important to continue to affirm and focus on the feeling and the situation that brings you that feeling of love. Continue to focus on the breath and allow it to move any discomfort out of your body. It will. Do this for five to ten minutes in the areas where you experience pain or illness. Let it be easy. It may take some time before you feel that anything is changing or coming to you. Don't stop or quit because you think you aren't doing it right. Spirit doesn't need you to do it right, it just needs you to be consistent and willing! It will do the rest. You are sending a very strong message to the physical, mental, emotional, and spiritual layers of your body. Every ounce of your being is engaged in telling your body and your soul that you are ready and willing to accept this and to change your reality and perception of yourself and the nature of God Spirit and life.

You are training yourself to learn to listen with your heart to your spirit and creation. The voice you hear coming from the Love Meditation will be different than the one that emanates from the mind (ego). The voice of the heart is the voice of your spirit and soul. If you are not used to listening from this place, it can take some practice.

Anywhere there is pain, tension, or illness there is a disruption in the flow of divine love (spirit and energy). By doing the Love Meditation daily, the love you give to yourself and body will restore the flow. Your willingness to affirm your full expression of divine love flowing through you will make it so, just as it did to remove all of the pain in the trigger points in my body.

If you'd like to have a recorded CD or mp3 of the Love Meditation to guide you in the meditation it is available on my website wwwsoullighthealingacademy.com.

CHAPTER TWELVE

Claim Your Freedom

If you are depressed, you are living in the past. If you are anxious, you are living in the future. If you are at peace, you are living in the present. —Lao Tzu

Most certainly, it isn't fun when we live with chronic pain or illness, and we dream of a time when we can be free of it. It may seem ridiculous to think about claiming your good, but this is going to be your new mindset. No one is going to hand it to you. You are going to have to claim your health, fun, and freedom.

Think about it: if you are living with chronic pain or illness, does it create limitations in your life and day-to-day living? For most people, the answer is an absolute "Yes," not to mention the fear that it creates. There were many places where I did not go and many things I did not do when I lived with chronic pain. I would try to plan things and do my best to have fun, but there was always an underlying fear just below the surface of my life. It wasn't until I started to reprogram my beliefs for a more positive existence that I was able to begin to dream of a different reality, one of joy and vitality.

As sad as it sounds to me now, I felt so unworthy of good things for most of my early years in life: happiness, financial freedom, sober friendships, a rewarding career, or vibrant health. To be honest, I was jealous of anyone who had these things, and I couldn't figure out how to get them. The message and belief that I had integrated firmly into my being was that I wasn't "good enough." I didn't believe in good things for *me*. Once I learned to rewire my brain and beliefs, I began to dream, to fake it until I could make it...and the Universe began to reward me with small opportunities and victories. There were many days that I reverted back to my old ways of thinking. I needed support to keep myself positive. I decided to make it into a fun game, instead of continuing to beat myself up every day with self-demeaning, self-deprecating thoughts.

Now more than ever, I feel this is a crucial piece of healing and creating a life of peace, health, happiness, and freedom. I challenge you to turn on the television and find anything other than sensationalized fear and negativity. The media and technology highway have programmed much of the world to live in constant fear of annihilation and illness. Even something as simple as a snow storm becomes apocalyptic. I, for one, watch little or no television because of the dark, depressive energy that most programming leaves me with. I encourage you to examine where in your life you could eliminate negative programming, situations, and people. It's time to replace them with positive programming that will help you create and attract fun, health, and freedom. I did not and could not sit around waiting for good things to drop in my lap, I had to claim them and go after them. I had to move in their direction, and most times that meant going against the grain and convention of doctors, the medical community, friends, family, and the media. Our life force, our spirit, our divinity are, as we've discussed, a field of loving energy, and we live in a "like attracts like" world of energy. The spiritual laws of the universe, as we also discussed, affect everyone, like gravity, whether or not we believe or understand its working principle. And so it is true that energy follows thought and *feeling.* What you think about and how you *feel* about those thoughts is what will create your present and your future.

I use two specific tools to reprogram my thoughts and to shift my feelings and emotions about myself and about the nature of life to be in alignment with the truth of spiritual principles and how God Spirit sees each of us in the world. They were pivotal in creating the peace, health, happiness, and freedom I desired.

The first is an exercise called "Claim Your Health and Freedom." Like meditation and the other tools in this section, it is important to do them consistently. It's like exercising—it cannot be stored up. In order to continue to see results, you must use these tools. Do not stop, even as you see progress and success. I still use these tools, not because I haven't progressed and healed, but because I am constantly evolving, changing, growing, and expanding into more and more of myself, and I want God Spirit to lead me every step of the way! What Spirit wants for you is greater than you can ever imagine for yourself.

Our ego mind likes to create limitations. But with these tools, we reprogram our mind and subconscious beliefs. That's what I did and what I continue to do today to create and attract the kinds of people, situations, circumstances, and life that I desire.

CLAIM YOUR FREEDOM

Write these statements every morning and every night for 28 days, (or longer if you like). These statements are general but life-affirming. I found or created ones that resonated with me (and that many of my clients have found effective). If you find ones that you feel resonate with you after the first 28 days, add or substitute them to the list, but continue to do the exercise every morning and every night. I like to do them first thing in the morning and then follow them with the 5-minute visualization that follows, below.

Write these statements every day and speak them out loud after you write them:[1]

1. The whole world loves me, serves me, nurtures me, and wants me to win.

---

[1]Affirmations 1, 2, 3, 9, 11, and 12 are adapted from *Dare to Claim Your Good! Prayer Statements for Unexpected Prosperity* by Edwene Gaines. Affirmations 6 and 7 are adapted from *Masterminding 101* by Mary Reynolds. Affirmations 10 and 13 are adapted from *Dynamic Laws of Prosperity* by Catherine Ponder.

2. I choose to release all sense of burden, struggle, and fear.

3. I choose to live in trust.

4. I am worthy and I expect great things to happen.

5. I am love so I feed myself loving thoughts.

6. Divine love flowing through me frees me from every negative influence.

7. All power is given me to control my thoughts, to vitalize my body, to experience success, and to bless others.

8. I am now creating radiant and vibrant health.

9. God provides lavishly for me and all of humanity.

10. I stir up the gifts of God within me and around me and I am blessed with happiness, health, and freedom.

11. I have wonderful gifts to give and I give generously.

12. I have wonderful gifts to receive and I receive joyously.

13. Divine love radiates through me and draws to me all that is needed to make me healthy, happy, and my life complete.

Keep a record of your surprises, synchronicities, and successes. Be aware of decreased pain or other symptoms.

VISUALIZATION

I had one driving force along my healing journey: I had a vision of being healthy and happy. No matter how dark it got, I held that vision in my heart. I just knew that I was going to move out of the place I was in. There had to be more to life than what I was experiencing. I didn't accept my circumstances. I dreamed of running and walking again. I didn't know how it would happen, but I pictured it over and over and over again. I didn't know how I would rid myself of all the symptoms of fibromyalgia, but I just couldn't and didn't accept it as my fate. I used to visualize myself *breaking free* from its grip, literally. The vision I used to see was emblazoned in my memory: I saw myself running across the finish line of a race, breaking through the ribbon, my arms outstretched, my whole body shining in victory and sunlight as I crossed the finish line. Freedom, success, health, and vitality were mine! I saw it and felt it with every ounce of my being. And on the day of that race, there were pink clouds in the sky! Pink clouds still follow me and protect me everywhere I go, floating over my head, reminding me of my greatness and divinity.

Today I help clients create and visualize their own finish line. It's so important to have a dream and a visualization to move toward. It creates hope and it helps Spirit work through you on your behalf. It lets Spirit know that you have *faith,* and as corny as it sounds, that is the faith moves mountains! It truly does.

So it's time to wake up your dream muscles! If you could be, do, or have anything, what would you imagine? How would you see yourself and your life five years from now? What would it look like? This is an exercise I have done many, many times to create a vision for what I wanted to bring into my life.

At first it wasn't easy. I had *no* idea what I wanted and I let my current circumstances confine what I thought was possible. But I got much better at this when I was able to be present in my body and my heart. Sure, there were times I talked myself out of things, but that's why it is so important to get into your heart and let God Spirit help you create your dreams and express your gifts, talent, passions, and purpose.

Start right now. Get your journal or notebook and write a letter to yourself. Date it five years from today's date. Describe your ideal scene as if it's already happened. For example, my first scene was one in which I was free from pain and I ran and practiced yoga every day. I had a fit, healthy body. I had a private practice helping others achieve their health goals. I lived debt-free and had more than enough money to do things I enjoyed. I had lots of fun, like-minded friends.

Every day when I did my Claim Your Freedom exercises, I visualized and imagined that scenario and that life for myself. I held that space of warmth and love in my heart while I imagined my ideal scene. From my ideal scene, a plan emerged and unfolded, and God Spirit put the right pieces, people, and circumstances in motion for me. That's not to say that I didn't have to take action; I did, but I learned to trust and move forward.

Before I knew it, my visualizations became my reality. Yours can too, but you have to create your dream and visualization first. The plan may change along the way, as God Spirit lines things up, but you have to start with the vision. It's like traveling across the country. You don't just get in your car and start driving. You make a plan. You have a dream and vision of where you'd like to go, the things you'd like to see and do. You pack a bag. You get the oil changed in your car. You get maps. You go to the bank. You have a plan to get from point A to point B. This is how you set things in motion for your health, happiness, and freedom too. You don't just sit back and pray, or hope that you'll get there. You plan and visualize. I can't emphasize enough how powerful these two exercises can be for creating a new reality.

CHAPTER THIRTEEN

Mala Meditation: Affirming and Shifting Your Reality

The first recipe for happiness: avoid too lengthy meditation on the past. —Andre Maurois

The mala meditation and tradition has been around for thousands of years, originating in the Hindu culture. Its traditional intentions are similar to the rosary beads of the Catholic tradition: to cleanse and purify negativity and to instill love and God-likeness in the beholder, at least that is my current interpretation. I have heard many evolved teachers and world-thought leaders say, "Take the best and leave the rest," and that is what I have done with the mala meditation. I have adapted it to serve the highest good and I personally don't get caught up in "should," statements, or restrictions. The following are some of the basic concepts of mala meditation from the Hindu culture, followed by a discussion of how I use the mala beads and meditation and how I have applied it for health, healing, and creating positive change.

A mala is a string of beads used to count mantras, or prayers, in sets of 108 repetitions. A mantra is a word or series of words spoken (chanted) aloud or silently to invoke spiritual qualities. Chanting is used as a spiritual tool in virtually every cultural and religious tradition. In the yogic tradition, a mantra is a Sanskrit word that is believed to have special power to transform consciousness, promote healing, or fulfill desires.

The practice of chanting a mantra can be used as a form of meditation. Sitting in a comfortable position, with the eyes closed, the mantra is repeated silently or aloud. The mind is focused on the mantra, the mind lets go of thought, and the breath naturally becomes slower and deeper. It is a wonderful way to create inner peace and reduce mental chatter.

In traditional mala meditations, we hold the string of mala beads in the right hand and use our thumb to "count" each mantra by touching the bead during the recitation, and then lightly pull the bead toward you on completion, moving to the next bead.

Mala beads can be made from any material, from sandalwood to gemstones and crystals. Some may be worn as a necklace or a bracelet. The large bead should not be counted during the meditation and is used as a starting and ending point of the recitation. If you have a wrist mala (bracelet) of 27 beads, you will need to repeat the mantra and move around the bracelet a total of four times to equal one round.

In my adaptation, I instruct students to do three full rounds (108 x 3) of prayer/affirmation. Each round consists of 108 recitations. This infuses the mala with energy and the intention of the prayer or affirmation. To empower the mala and the mantra used, I recommend practicing the mantra each day for 40 continuous days. When the mala becomes empowered, it can be worn or lightly placed on oneself or others to transmit the energy of the mantra, as well as the energetic qualities of the mala. When you use a new mantra with a mala, this energy becomes replaced by the new mantra.

Beautiful gemstone mala beads use the power and intentions of crystals to help raise the energy and vibration of the mantras. Many say that the malas should remain at home in a sacred space, but I have chosen to always wear my mala beads to feel that they are infusing my intentions and love into my body and life, and out into the world as well. I have found the mala meditation to be an amazingly powerful tool for creating change and healing!

Over the years I've had many clients tell me that this process seemed "weird" or a little "out there," yet they didn't have any resistance to the idea of rosary beads. The Catholics actually adopted the rosary from Hindu culture. I encourage you to be open to these new ideas and processes. They changed my life!

If you do what you've always done, you'll get what you've always gotten. Are you willing to take action? Are you willing to take 100 percent responsibility and be consistent in showing up for yourself? Are you willing to be okay with who you are and not succumb to other people's beliefs (especially *well-meaning* friends and family members)?

I have to admit that when I first started down this road, it felt awkward. There wasn't nearly as much support readily available as there is today. These sorts of things were hippie-ish and considered *New Age, weird,* and *wicky-woo.* They were definitely not in the realm of medicine. But when new thought leaders like Deepak Chopra, MD brought these traditions to the mainstream with science and research, folks began to embrace their value. Now, more than ever, it's not weird. Own it and appreciate it. Don't assume that it has no validity for health and healing just because it wasn't prescribed by your doctor.

Below are the three mantras I use and have adapted to fit my beliefs and needs. Depending on what you desire to change or bring into your life, you will create your own "fill in the blank" intention and affirmation for each of the three mantras. I have given you examples of what mine were when I was working on my health.

1. Dear God Spirit, I am one with you. Thank you for dissolving (fill in the blank). *Repeat 108 times, one full round of the mala beads.*
2. Dear God Spirit, I am one with you. Thank you for blessing me with (fill in the blank). *Repeat 108 times, one full round of the mala beads.*
3. Dear God Spirit, I am one with you. Thank you for granting me (fill in the blank). *Repeat 108 times, one full round of the mala beads.*

When I was doing this mala meditation for healing, my "fill-in the blanks" went something like this:

1. Dear God Spirit, I am one with you. Thank you for dissolving my fear and pain.
2. Dear God Spirit I am one with you. Thank you for blessing me with perfect health.
3. Dear God Spirit, I am one with you. Thank you for granting me vitality and aligning my highest good.

I did each of the three mantras 108 times around the full strand of mala beads. I visualized the mantra affirmations as if they had already happened. While saying the words and visualizing the end result I wanted, I looked contrary to my current reality and drew into my heart and mind's eye a life full of self-love and being loved by the whole world.

If any voice came in to tell me otherwise, I "sent it away"—literally! I would say out loud, "I send you away. You are not God and you are not my reality," and I used the mantras and visualizations to reprogram myself, my world, my beliefs, my subconscious, and my reality. It worked for me and it can work for you.

The problem is that most people stop just before the changes are about to occur. When things don't go *exactly* as you plan, let them go; something better is on the way. So many times I clung to situations and people that weren't right for me and I knew it but I did it because I was afraid of the unknown. Embrace the unknown. Allow Spirit as many opportunities as possible to work through you.

CHAPTER FOURTEEN

Digestion: The Metaphor of Life

Let food be thy medicine and medicine be thy food.

—Hippocrates

U p until this point, all of my suggestions have been more of an energetic and spiritual nature, and you may be wondering about some of the more tangible things that you can do to create health and healing. The most important place for you to focus on, after learning to bring the first four tools into your life, is digestion and nutrition. After all, everything we put into our body is raw material for our cells.

I cannot talk about healing and reversing fibromyalgia without addressing digestion. I have to say, after chronic pain and cancer remission, chronic digestive problems are probably the number one health challenge I have helped people with in my private coaching practice. Digestive problems can not only put a real cramp in one's lifestyle and quality of life, but they can also be the physical cause of many degenerative illnesses. So many important functions of life happen in our abdomen and solar plexus energy center.

Our digestive tract is so much more than just a powerhouse of cellular activity. It is also a spiritual metaphor for life. In addition to feeding ourselves organic, whole food nutrition, there are a few spiritual principles that can heal the digestive disorders that tend to accompany chronic illness or pain. If you suffer with any sort of digestive problem and are taking medication for it, either prescription or over the counter drugs, there are a few things you should know that could heal and reverse the problem completely.

From an energetic and spiritual perspective, we can heal numerous chronic problems by looking at specific areas of the digestive process to get answers on which areas of our lives have broken down. When I first began to access my gifts as a medical intuitive, I would get concrete and specific insights and messages into the emotional and spiritual causes of people's physical illnesses. I would know things like: a patient's ulcer was caused by the unresolved anger and resentment she held toward her brother. It was literally eating away at her because she felt that her sibling was putting her down all the time. No amount of dietary changes or Nexium can repair that. As soon as she's willing to accept 100 percent responsibility for the situation, healing could begin.

Our digestive tract, from beginning to end, is a direct metaphor for life. When we look at how we handle life in general, we receive information and energy on a daily, minute-to-minute basis; that is the taking in of "food." We use our teeth (mind, body, and spirit) to chew up the information, to break it down into smaller pieces so that we can "swallow it": a sort of pre-digestive process. If we don't break it down into smaller pieces or if we eat too quickly, what happens? We get indigestion, upset stomach. Everywhere we look in our culture we can find literal translations regarding our gut feelings, the emotional and energetic components associated with digestion.

Once we have broken down "life" into smaller pieces and made it easy to swallow, it goes down through sphincters and valves to enter the stomach, where digestive fluids and enzymes (our fire, passions, and emotions) can continue to break down nutrients and information intended to support and nourish us in life, our purpose, and physical well-being. Different enzymes are responsible for breaking down different nutrients and sending them to the appropriate areas. From there, the micronutrients leave the stomach to enter the large and small intestines, the place where the nutrients can be delivered, and whatever doesn't nurture and serve us can move through easily and effortlessly to be removed as "waste."

So this is our process of life and digestion. Where has digestion broken down when there is a digestive illness? This can give us insight into where we are not effectively processing information (like perceived traumatic events, or negative energy from our boss). Are you having problems with your teeth, indicating a problem in breaking down or forming new core beliefs about ourselves and our life, chewing up information? Or is there are problem with reflux, where we are burning mad at something that has become too much to keep down? Or perhaps a problem with blood sugar and diabetes shows up because life has become filled with sorrow and we can't find a little sweetness to life?

What I came to understand when I was living with digestive problems, and what I have observed from hundreds of my clients living with digestive problems, is that most of the time the illness has manifested as the result of emotional or physical trauma or a perceived threat to their safety and survival. When one feels violated or traumatized, difficult emotions can get stored somewhere along the physical and metaphorical digestive process and can get stuck in the tissues of the digestive tract.

In the chakra energy system I spoke of previously, the digestive process affects our throat chakra (expression), the solar plexus chakra that processes energies related to our self-esteem, and of course the heart center and how we perceive ourselves. Lastly, it affects our root chakra, our safety, security, and survival. It is not uncommon to see any or all of these areas affected when a trauma has occurred, but with this metaphor we are able to see more closely which area has "broken down" in the process.

There are certainly times when we need to have life-saving surgery or take medications to manage acute symptoms, but to stop there is to do ourselves a great injustice and disservice. There will never be enough pills, surgery, chemotherapy, or radiation to make up for the fact that we are storing emotional pain or trauma in the cells and tissues of our body. We must be willing to feed ourselves *love*. This is how I not only healed, but reversed, the physical symptoms in my body. On a spiritual and emotional level, I learned to feed myself love! You can too.

We've all heard stories about the person who *did everything right* and ended up with a terminal illness. They ate super healthy and exercised regularly. They followed all of the "shoulds" that modern medicine and experts prescribed, and yet they got cancer. What went wrong? What I have witnessed is that without addressing these emotional and spiritual aspects that are repressed in our bodies, there is no amount of pills or nutritional supplements that can make up for being unwilling to feed ourselves love, on every level.

With current medical models, we take Nexium and Prilosec for the physical symptoms and we believe that our bodies do not know how to digest our food properly, but this is not the truth. Doctors don't address the underlying emotions and fears created from trauma. Feelings of abandonment, unworthiness, anger, or fear can be stored in the gut for many years. On a subconscious level, we aren't even aware that we've buried them there until they literally "come up." This is why the Love Meditation is so effective at healing any area of the body.

We can eat all the broccoli and red peppers that we can take into our mouths, but if we can't digest it because we're still holding a negative emotion from something that happened five minutes or five years ago, it won't be able to nourish us. In order to heal I had to use love to release the emotions buried in the trigger points. What are you holding onto that could be stored in your digestive tract or other tissues in the body? I have not met one living soul who can't benefit from letting go of old emotions and resentments.

Healing the digestive tract is not about the "shoulds" and dictates of doctors, nutritionists, pharmaceutical companies, modern scientific studies, and the billion-dollar supplement industry, but the "food" that we feed our bodies with our minds. With our thoughts, fears, and emotions, we cut ourselves off from our peace, health, and happiness. We support ourselves to be nourished on all levels when we learn not to make choices from love instead of our fear-full places.

We must become comfortable with feeding ourselves love and making it a priority. When we cannot do this, we put ourselves low on our own priority list and that creates illness. At every class or workshop I teach I begin with a centering mediation and prayer, then participants "check in" to tell the group about their successes and triumphs in the last week. One woman in our class declared she was "too busy to do the Love Meditation." She did not make excuses. She honestly said, "I didn't even try. *Life* got in the way." While I respect her honesty, this is a very common lament I hear—people living lives of pain, illness, and quiet desperation, unable to give themselves five minutes of uninterrupted self-care each morning and evening. I personally believe that nothing in life is so important that it should prevent you from taking five minutes for yourself twice a day. Unless the house is on fire, nothing keeps me from my daily meditation. To feed, nurture, and nourish myself is the ultimate act of self-love. Anything less is an act of self-denial that has gone on far too long and is, I believe, the major cause of pain and illness.

If we are to be a part of a collective healing for ourselves and for the world, we must learn to put ourselves and our well-being first. It's like they tell us on the airplane: put the oxygen mask on yourself first, then tend to those in the seat next to you. In order to heal we must be willing to give ourselves, first and foremost, extreme self-care.

When we are able to acknowledge the divine order of our physical bodies, we are able to see that God created our bodies as vessels for the animated spirit to experience the full expression of his goodness. With this awareness it becomes so much easier to treat our bodies well and to feed them well. We can let go of all the "shoulds" when we love ourselves from the inside out. We no longer live in fear of following the next fad diet to get healthy or avoid cancer. You'll learn, as I did, to listen to your own needs without needing someone else to tell you what to eat. It's what I like to call being an intuitive eater, and it creates peace and ease in your life. Think about it: how much stress is created by the confusion from all the diet books and information flooding the mass markets? Nearly every day on the evening news there is a report that says, "Researchers at such and such university have found that coffee (or some other food) can prevent cancer," and six months later another study reports that it causes dementia or heart attacks. So are we left to pick our poisons according to which ailment we prefer?

I have helped thousands of clients learn to change their meal plans and eat meals according to the seasons and their geographic location. We live in a world of hurry up-24/7-overconsumption. Grocery stores market to a sense of affluence in which everything is shipped in from around the world, and we can obtain anything we want at any time of the year. Many people have forgotten how to eat with their instincts and intuition for their region and the seasons. On all levels, stop and ask yourself, am I feeding myself love? With my thoughts, with my actions, am I feeding myself love? Feed yourself love.

If you're not willing to feed yourself love, you're not willing to acknowledge your divinity. You are denying every aspect of God Spirit and the energy of its very creation, of our bodies, and everything on our planet.

As a holistic practitioner I have never been a big advocate of taking a lot of herbs and supplements. There are times when they are needed and a good *short-term* solution, such as for imbalances like seasonal colds. But God made bodies that know how to heal and that gravitate toward being fed and nurtured with food in its purest and most naturally high vibration. Yes, like everything else on this planet, your food has a vibration. Real food is alive and packed with nutrients. It has a high vibration. Processed and packaged foods filled with pesticides and preservatives have vibrations that are not similar to our bodies and can cause detriment. Remember, like attracts like. High vibration foods create high vibration healthy minds and bodies.

Instinctively, even before I became a holistic practitioner and nutritional specialist, I felt that Mother Nature created what we need to nourish ourselves, that plants were designed to feed and nourish our bodies, and that we should get most of our nutrients from real, live, whole foods as much as possible. The micronutrients in the "whole" provide things that pills and powders can't. That is, fresh ground turmeric will always be better than a turmeric capsule. I have also taught thousands of clients about my "good, better, best" philosophy when it comes to nutrition, supplements, and healing.

I recommend a seasonal, Ayurvedic meal plan to my private clients and work to teach them seasonal nutrition based on their body type, current geographical location, and life stage. That is, a menopausal woman with fibromyalgia living in California would get different nutrition recommendations from me than a woman with fibromyalgia living in Vermont who is 28 years old.

The best possible chance that anyone has for correcting and healing digestive problems is to integrate a good, sound, seasonal nutritional plan based on whole foods, while addressing emotional and spiritual aspects of life challenges. In my experience, one without the other does not produce lasting results.

CHAPTER FIFTEEN

Wisdom of the World's First Medicine

When diet is wrong, medicine is of no use. When diet is correct, medicine is of no need. —Ayurvedic proverb

A s you read previously, my healing path at Kripalu led me to an amazing system of medicine and healing called Ayurveda. The literal Hindu translation of Ayurveda is *science of life*. It is believed to be the first system of medicine and healing in the world, dating back some 5000 years. It has had such a profound effect on my life and the life of my clients that it would be a disservice for me not to include a brief introduction of its benefits for all those wishing to enjoy health, happiness, and inner peace.

As with everything I have studied in my life, I have learned to *take the best and leave the rest*. Ayurveda has much wisdom and many tools that can benefit us in the twenty-first century, but I don't believe that we should make ourselves stressed and rigid trying to adopt every single aspect of a massive ancient system and culture to our modern-day world.

A basic knowledge and understanding can help you make good choices for yourself based on your body-mind type, called a "dosha" in Ayurveda. I have seen far too many clients give up on making positive changes with principles of Ayurveda because they felt overwhelmed by the vast amount of information What I recommend is to learn a basic understanding of what Ayurveda has to offer. It offers profound insight into the workings of our body, mind, and spirit, accompanied by a "road map" of three individual body types and guidelines of how to keep them in balance. Its core principles are based on the elements we find in nature. They are present in every aspect of nature; therefore, because we *are* these elements, these principles of balance apply to everything we do in our lives.

I have been practicing and using the principles of Ayurveda in my daily living for nearly twenty years. I have shared its benefits with clients, friends, and family for almost as long, and I continue to marvel at the consistent and tangible healing that can occur from implementing its simple and easy practices. Perhaps that is why so many don't embrace it, like the Love Meditation—it seems too simple and too good to be true or effective. We like to complicate things.

I'll share with you the beginner's mind approach to principles of Ayurveda, along with a few examples of how clients have used them to reverse and heal illness.

We see the elements of nature everywhere we look, and our bodies are no different. Like the different parts of the world, we all have a predominance of elements that make up our nature. In the tropics we find heat and moisture, in the southwest United States we find heat and dryness, in Alaska we find cold and dry, and in Spain, we find yet another environment. In each of these places we find crops and foods that grow best in certain climates and conditions, and so it is with our bodies and our minds using the principles of Ayurveda. When we work with the elements, we thrive. When we work against them, over time we will find that imbalances begin to set in. So how can we use these principles to reverse illness and enhance health and well-being? It's actually simple. We look to the universal principle of "like attracts like" and we counter imbalances with opposite qualities. Okay, let's put this into tangible terms.

There are three main body-mind types in Ayurveda. I caution you, however, not to label yourself into a category like we do with a diagnosis in Western medicine. The Ayurvedic body-mind types are *guidelines*, and like everything else in life, should remain fluid. The beauty of Ayurveda is that it thrives in flexibility and intuition, and nothing is carved in stone. Release the idea that you have to "get it right" or that you can just do "this" or "that" one time and you'll arrive at your prefect destination. Ayurveda is much more like peeling back the layers of an onion.

The three body types are represented by the elements of nature and the proportions and predominance of each element in your body and mind. You have *all* of the elements within your blueprint, but you are born with a predominance that characterizes how you and your body and mind move through and relate to life, including nutrition, sleep, activity, weather preferences, work environment, digestion, and mental processes, to name a few. The three body-mind types and their corresponding elements are:

Vata: air and ether

Pitta: fire and water

Kapha: earth and water

You may be thinking, as I did twenty years ago, Big deal, so what does that mean for me? What it means is that these elements are active in every aspect of your body, mind, and being. When you understand how they *show up* and what you are doing to either keep them in balance or throw them out of balance, you can determine how to make corrections so you live with peace, health, and happiness. Each dosha has certain characteristics and tendencies that will surface when it goes out of balance. Like a little red flag, if you are aware of your dosha, its tendencies, and how to pacify them, you'll be able to ward off illness and imbalance with food choices and daily routines that counter the "like attracts like" principles.

For example, in Ayurveda we distinguish between the body types when treating arthritis. The underlying causes of a Vata-type arthritis are different than those of a Pitta-type arthritis. Vata-type arthritis is characterized by dryness in the body and a lack of synovial fluid to lubricate the joints and tissues. It is characterized by cold, popping, cracking joints, and is worse during winter or for those living in cool climates. We treat it by adding warmth and moisture to the body with food qualities and oil massages that penetrate nutrients into the skin and joints. We also recommend personal care and body treatments that can be done by the client at home and are cost-effective, putting the responsibility and outcome of reversal in the hands of the client. For Pitta-type arthritis we do the same thing, but that type of arthritis is characterized by too much heat and swelling in the body; the focus then is on cooling and reducing the stiffness caused by the swelling. We focus on nutrition that pulls heat out of the body and joints and cools the liver.

A client once came to me who believed, after watching the Dr. Oz show, that she was doing everything right and everything she could to treat her arthritis symptoms naturally. Yet in reality, according to Ayurvedic principles for her specific body type, she was actually antagonizing her symptoms and her body. Without knowing her Ayurvedic body type and its inherent characteristics, she was actually doing more harm than good. With a few simple changes she found nearly instant relief, and over time when she continued these steps she found complete reversal of her pain and symptoms She was shocked to learn that the things she was doing that seemed healthy were actually making things worse. If you continue to do something and don't find relief or reversal of symptoms, even if it's "natural," then it isn't working.

This particular woman was a Vata type and she was suffering with Vata arthritis symptoms. At our initial consultation, even before getting into a full assessment and evaluation, I could see that she was very dry. Her skin, lips, and mouth/speech were dry. When I examined her nutrition plan, I discovered that she was drinking five to six cups of green tea every day because she had seen on the television program that green tea was high in antioxidants and had anti-inflammatory properties, thinking that both should improve her condition. The client complained to me that she drank tons and tons of water every day and still had dry mouth and never seemed to quench her thirst. She was also taking large amounts of turmeric in capsule supplement form, again because the television program revered it for its anti-inflammatory properties.

Now here is how I looked at these aspects from an Ayurvedic and energetic approach. Green tea, like all teas, is astringent, which also makes it drying. Despite the fact that it has antioxidant properties, it was causing severe dryness in her entire body. Since she is Vata type, already characterized by dryness, this was essentially making the lack of lubrication in her joints even worse. The large quantities of turmeric were also doing the same thing. Turmeric is astringent as well as cooling. It is wonderful for cleansing the liver and blood, but with long-term use in large quantities it can become too cooling and drying for Vata types who have tendencies toward cool and dry, inherent in their body type. In addition to this was the fact that she lived in a region that has long, cold, dry winters...and, well, you get the idea. All of these factors were contributing to making her symptoms worse rather than better, which is why she was desperate to try Ayurveda and something new. She was at her wits' end and had tried "everything else."

I recommended that she stop taking the supplements and tea. We started her on glucosamine and chondroitin supplements to add lubrication to the joints and synovial fluid. She followed a Vata pacifying diet for six months, eating warm, moist foods like oatmeal, soups, and stews, and avoiding cold, dry foods like salads and crackers. She added more good-quality oils, (coconut, olive, and ghee to her diet), and she did a daily self-massage on her hands and affected joints with an herbal-infused oil. She took one Ayurvedic supplement with meals to improve digestion and absorption of nutrients from her food. Within one week she reported improvement of her symptoms. Within six months she was free from arthritic joint pain following this regime (and of course, doing the Love Meditation).

This woman's case is not unique. With Ayurveda, I find improvement in nearly every single client's conditions when they learn the basics of their body-mind type and how to work with it in all stages of the life cycle, especially for woman in menopause. It is not magic. It just takes a commitment and responsibility on the part of the client, but only a rare few who have explored Ayurveda have not met with delight and success. I highly recommend you learn the basics and work with a qualified and certified practitioner. It provides a great opportunity to become empowered and to truly understand yourself.

CHAPTER SIXTEEN

This Life is for You

I have found that if you love life, life will love you back. —Arthur
Rubinstein

It is my deepest desire that you have found an opening or slight glimmer of hope in these pages that will lead you from pain or illness to become your own healer. My intention is to assist you in finding the truth of your divinity, and to restore the flow of divine love to your body, life, and being. It was an incredible path that led me out of chronic pain, suffering, and illness, and I sincerely believe that yours can happen much more quickly than mine did with the tools and wisdom offered here.

You are meant to live a life of health, happiness, and inner peace. It is for you. It is for everyone. Give yourself permission. Give yourself love. Give yourself the means and the tools to live as the full expression of God, regardless of what others may tell you, regardless of what others may think is possible. This is YOUR life. Do not deny yourself the health and well-being you deserve because you are concerned that you'll be judged. I wasted so much time and energy worrying about being accepted and judged for my beliefs and experiences, and for the path that God had planned for me. Wow, was I wrong! The life I live with eternal spirit, energy, love, and God in the driver's seat is so much better than I could have ever planned with my fearful ego mind.

You are loved. Your life is divine. You are surrounded by miracles. Accept yourself. Love yourself. Believe, really believe, that you can have the health and life that you want. It's waiting for you. Accept your miracle, today.

With love, I wish you peace, health, and happiness.

RESOURCES

Healing Touch Program
15439 Pebble Gate
San Antonio, TX 78232
www.healingtouchprogram.com

RECOMMENDED READING

Mind over Medicine by Lissa Rankin

Dying to Be Me by Anita Moorjani

Of Monkeys and Dragons by Michelle Longo O'Donnell

When the Wolf is at the Door by Michelle Longo

O'Donnell *Only Receive* by Michelle Longo O'Donnell